FAMILY GUIDE

FAMILY GUIDE

ON LOVE, COURT-SHIP, SEX
AND MARRIAGE
PLUS
POST MARRIAGE
&
MISCELLANEOUS ITEMS.

Dee Hoodith

authorHOUSE®

AuthorHouse™
1663 Liberty Drive
Bloomington, IN 47403
www.authorhouse.com
Phone: 1-800-839-8640

First published by AuthorHouse   05/23/2011

ISBN: 978-1-4634-1269-2 (sc)
ISBN: 978-1-4634-1268-5 (dj)
ISBN: 978-1-4634-1267-8 (ebk)

Library of Congress Control Number: 2011908663

Printed in the United States of America

Any people depicted in stock imagery provided by Thinkstock are models, and such images are being used for illustrative purposes only.

Certain stock imagery © Thinkstock.

This book is printed on acid-free paper.

CONTENTS

The Book "FAMILY Guide"

Chapters

Love, Courtship & Marriage, Sex plus Post Marriage

Purpose

The involvement of man and woman, for unification and satisfaction of passionate love and for the choosing of a lifelong partner, is based step by step in the herein-presented order.

With caution and wisdom, sex should be enjoyed and flavored with ecstasy (exalted state of feelings), without depression, worry and negative concern.

Playful teasing can and will accentuate the enjoyment, but it must also be carefully controlled because it intensifies the human sex urge and can be tolerated only to a point, thereafter it would explode as an atomic bomb.

Because of the beauty of this work, which is so great, I want each person to be an owner of it. To some, it may be sweet and not only impressive, but interesting. However, to all my readers, I do only wish you successful love and togetherness, but that one of the greatest opportunity still open to you and it is to give or ask as many questions that maybe, bothering you, while you however, know that all the answers can be found in this very book, if you look diligently.

Science will never stop working in this or any other field. Congratulation to them all, but this common sense would no doubt, prove best than them all.

Briefing About The Author

I was born the third in line of two elder, a sister and a brother and following me was three other sisters of our parents, who loved and cared for us all equally.

My birth was on Wednesday the 20th of November 1963. I grew up at my birthplace Guyana. After school years, I happened to be employed. I give birth to my son and shortly after, I relocate to the United State of America. I however kept furthering my studies. I have attained an Associate of Science Degree and a Bachelor's of Science Degree in Finance, graduating with the Magna Cum Laude honors. Then came along my two daughters, together with my three children and husband, life went on as the tide, some days up, sometimes down.

This book is dedicated to
William H. Hoodith
Who passed on in March 2008.
With his Knowledge, experience and Know-how
Has helped me to bring this book to light.

PREFACE

I am aware, that I cannot please all my readers on this work but for sure, I have brought out new facts and ideas to you here. At some point you shall learn some things you did not know. New light has shone in this direction and by this way; it is my aim and objective in educating you. So, at least, I feel that I have gained and made headway, if it can be considered part of the way, if not the whole.

Be fair in your critics, by bringing to my attention those weaknesses that you may find. Further, I wish to invite not only your criticism but also comments and questions on what more you would have expected in this work. I do not have the so-called educated ones in mind, but rather to the uneducated in this field of bliss and, help to save many a broken love affairs, where youth and inexperience are the faults and also to avoid or lessen the cause of many broken marriages.

The section which deals with tradition is included, not because I wish to propagate this sort of belief, but rather to update you of its existence and its acceptance anywhere you go. Whether you accept it or not, it will still be there to the end of time. So, the best thing is for you to have a basic knowledge of things in circulation.

The fruit of my labor is now laid before you, because of the knowledge bequest to you my readers. You have more facilities to learn this pleasurable art than others do. It is a game that contains much playfulness that it may appear to many as a novel. However, the truth conveyed through these simple actions, is as aged as the world. They are so simple that they may be disregarded and discarded as by some useless. However, they continue to this day and will continue to command the un-accomplished attention of wiser heads than yours and mine to the end of time, since man and woman, as lovers will be around.

It is for you to decide in this field whether you will direct or be directed, command or be commanded and as to whether you want to rise or fall. If you pre-judge this work by self-esteem, stubbornness and with an arrogant, hasty disposition, then you cannot be commander and you must consider whether you want to lead or be led, to toy someone or for someone to make you a toy and for you to seek someone or for someone to seek after you.

If you put forth effort to cultivate and be motivated to put into motion, this inborn power, which is within your reach. Then the door to success is in front of you. Hence, the door to happiness, it is for you to grasp the opportunity to open it and don't permit someone else to do so.

What I present to you in this book is the simple entrance into the art of practice and the extract of mysterious wonders in the sublime silver lining of love. Young lovers, be explorer and awake from the slumber of impossibilities and plunge into the refreshing bath of love and take a long and satisfying draught thereof, and thus, quench the burning heat from love. I am not delivering a discourse, instead I instruct.

I am not here as a preacher but as a teacher, so facts are not neglected because I leave the land of theory and enter into the realm of physical practice with tender and artful manipulations, where patience and perseverance are the price of success.

Remember the instructions and ideas herein before you, is the foundation over which I built my structure and so can you, with success. It is the key and without it, the door of love, which lies in the heart of the lovers, will not be opened to each other. You want to be a master and not a servant because the servant looks to the master for supply and so, many will look towards you for guidance, plus love and satisfaction. Your personal love magnetism as a master is that quality in which you attract interest, confidence, friendship and love. This is your secret of success coupled with politeness, which is the oil that lubricates society.

I welcome you to this comforting atmosphere, perfumed with the fragrance of spotless and undefiled love, as the scenery presented on a fair evening of the setting sun, viewed as an unforgettable scene by two young lovers' arms-in-arms, making love.

CHAPTER 1

The Treasure

This book is one of practical experience. You must read it with some measure of seriousness, with the determination to make use of the appreciated or selected information's disclosed to you. It should not be read for fun or past-the-time, although you may find some sections interested in this direction, less it will be of little value and it is then better to turn to some novel, if your study will chiefly be for amusement.

Practice makes perfect, so you sit behind the driving wheel, please obey the traffic rules and signs, so as to avoid accidents. Remember that you cannot "done the world" but you will go and leave all that you came and meet in it.

It is a new recipe for those who never knew about it. It is not a new discovery or credit, but a venture to put the tits and bits that are existing, but however are sleeping and to bring them out to your inquisitive mind's reach in writing. So, that they could no longer be over-looked but would stir the minds to a greater never done scope.

I have no intention in this work to replace previous medical professional books on these subjects, but rather to contribute and support those earlier scientific writers from a practical observation of a layman. The more you read about these matters I guess the more you will build or expand your knowledge and only after some wise application that you have read, you will come to appreciate this valuable and indispensable book.

I assure you, it may even challenge you. At some section of this book, you will learn something new, regardless of how intelligent you may be. You cannot know if it is sweet, palatable or has the right blend, unless you taste of its contents. I suggest that you do so greedily and unhesitatingly before it is too late.

This book is prepared to assist the lovers, both men and women to mold and trim the life partner into idea and real one, who was once imaginary and a dream of your sleeping life. Many persons who read parts of my manuscripts expressed in no uncertain terms their regrets for not having the opportunity of this type of knowledge brought out herein, and so, urge me to hasten up the completion of this book, which you now have in your hands.

The title "FAMILY GUIDE" was carefully considered and selected. However, it must not be misunderstood and so, expect it to be a general guide to the family. Its scope is limited to guide the family on Love, Courtship, Marriage, Sex and Post marriage, along with a few back-up services which are of relevant interest.

If one were to generalize on this title, then it would found to be wide as the universe and rolling stone, because life itself and all attachments need guides and have no ending.

You will appreciate, then the enormity of this impossible task of presenting to my readers, volumes of Family Guides to cover the variety of fields that goes to make life successful or unsuccessful. Although, I am somewhat limited, the topics treated in this work have covered a wide range and provides enough to fill you with the knowledge and to lead a successful life in the now and possible the hereafter. And should it serve its intended purpose, then there shall be no regrets, other than this book should have been yours, long before now. Anyway, it's not late for you to adjust yourself to corrective measures as provided, you can make the remaining allotted period, a happy and successful one.

Those who have passed on before without it have already gone, but it is with you in your hands, therefore, make the full use of it the best as you can. Take it with you (not necessary the book), the knowledge therein, wherever you go, even to the end of your journey.

The given advice's have penetrated all barriers, such as race, color, religion and politics and tries to foster the understanding that a women must respect herself as a wife and to take the place, inclusive of her husband and that the husband duly responsible for her. Also, a husband must respect himself as a husband and his wife as being responsible for him. The one true ground must be dwelled upon, by both parties and regarded as "holy ground".

No party is to feel superior above the other, nor does that he or she know all and everything. There should be sharing of opinions and consultations or at least, each other are to be up dated in such areas as seen fit and necessary. A family code of conduct is important and will be helpful. Do not set aside verbal communications in a pleasant atmosphere, for it is a compass and a charging system, whereby, you could have your read-off if you are a good pilot.

From all appearances, the human race is covetous and will remain so, because it is the only machine at man's disposal that propels him and cause him not to be static. How then, can you be stagnated, when there is life in you? Are you not going to hold your end in this game of LOVE, and get along to win a gold medal?

Some say that the forbidden fruit is the passion fruit, be it what it may, I disagree that it is a forbidden fruit. But however agrees that it is the passion fruit. The iceman in his advertisement says "cool-down". When you would have drunk the ice he sells but this treats the heat only, while LOVE removes both heat and passion. It takes two, it gives two and it satisfies two.

Please read your compass right, to be on course and no man or woman should have the cause to complain against each other's habits after reading this work, for it will refresh you and cool you down and also mold you for the future role as a true friend.

Should you by chance, come across any part of this book inappropriate, I wish to apologize for it. I have no intention to be disrespectful, disgraceful or being vulgar. I have had thorough and indebt knowledge into my writing, that to my opinion is the best and attractive enough to stimulate and assist those who did not know the missing parts of this puzzle of life. Neither evil, nor harm is meant but rather, total good, for these facts are the plain truth from experience and experiments.

CHAPTER 2

Confidence, your Key To Success

My aim also in this book, is a definite one, in which I hope to help you reach out towards a happier, lustrous and more productive life which no doubt, worth living, for after all your horizon is brighter than ever thought, don't remain blind. Look beyond your distance, and you will find that there are several paths you can take on this journey. Be positive, have fate and all other missing links will be created with confidence. Confidence is and has always been the key to success.

This book is a voyage of discoveries; by awakening your own potentials that are asleep in you and it is a great adventure, rather than you no doubt, bugged-down in frustration with the many unnecessary problems. Please see it as the greatest treasure house, a vault of loving togetherness of man and woman, the best of god's creation. Is it not a fantastic accomplishment? For we were not placed on this planet to stagnate but to actively live on and our stay is limited. Therefore, why not enjoy being here than to condemn yourself.

Sex, was formerly a sinful word to use but today, it is fashionable and most frequently used, and it also being taught in schools with success. Many however, feel it is getting wise too young. Sex is not skin deep—that is color, clothes and appearance, it should be deeper than your strong emotional qualities disclosed as a charitable gift of sympathy and understanding rather than money. A hit and run man or woman looks for physical qualities and money. But in looking for a life partner, he or she looks for a person with a heart and although beauty and money are an important role, today matured people looks beyond that, for Love, loyalty and or peace and appearance.

You are in the game, all the time and you are the main actor on stage. You no longer feel helpless with stage fright and nervousness, but rather I lead you up to explore the joy of this world, with the caution of not destroying yourself from greed. To feel that life is good, then you must give to life and it will give back to you compensatively.

While reading, are you not thrilled with sexual emotions, triggered by the mental telepathy (actions of the mind to another distance away). The negative mental vibration is a force, which penetrates beyond the physical body slowly and unerringly, it builds up or tears down knowingly or unknowingly the whole moral fabric of our being.

The hurry habit must weigh against its failures and success and should be avoided in the art of lovemaking. It is better to decline things than to leave unfinished or badly done tasks. Doubt, is the old man of the sea that we accept to be constant, maybe unaware, carrying about on our backs and it bars the way to accomplishment. What are the possibilities? Please remember whatever in nature is thine own, is floating in the air or sealed in stone. It shall raise the hills and swim the sea and like your shadow, follows you. A happy heart creates a cheerful appearance, but by sorrow of heart, the spirit is broken. Likewise a merry heart does great like medicine, but a broken spirit dry the bones. So please cultivate cheerfulness, if you want to be happy and gay. Even, our health depends, feeds and is nourished by it.

Know thyself, is a great and encouraging watch-word in this field and in this chapter. The foundation of heaven and hell is laid in man's own soul. So, faith is that magnet, which unites man more and more to the center of life and love. Obedience to good thoughts is liberty while discontent is a managed web of faith and doubt in the soul of man.

The tree of knowledge grows beside the tree of life, which is faith, itself. Man does not know his mental strength. Man does not on this planet aim to live alone, but to live well and draw from this fountain the sum of happiness for which this whole world strives. This includes all those who are given the luxury and sensual pleasures (voluntary) who easily lose his way, the religious and philosophical idealist in radiance of light who sees only love in their path.

You must separate your thoughts from the idea, that peace; love and happiness do not belong to your earth life, but the celestial hemisphere only. Just forget your troubles and worries dispose of them, banish them away to the deep sea of nothingness and continue to live as though nothing had crossed your path.

Some of your greatest enemies are false and double-cross friends and they are: jealousy, selfishness, covetousness, undue sensitiveness, morbid meditation, brooding, seclusiveness, worry, despondency and excess. These, and such other negatives, must be interrupted and checked before they make a mental and moral wreck of their victims.

To my opinion, if given the opportunity to be of service, I would consider it an ideal privilege for you to contribute with input or reliability, integrity and perseverance, not only to fill the desired post (sexual desires) but to acquire the esteemed required skills, patience, inclusive of confidence, loyalty, faithfulness and sincerity, which are all necessary as your prescription in the specifics. I shall look forward for your kind and courteous approach and consideration and possibly sure success in all your endeavors and undertakings in the herein mentioned field, as treated in this book.

I am sure, very often you have seen the hypocrite's discreet but yet mocking smile and you can also detect the hidden sob of a broken-hearted, whose dreams of happiness crumbled away before their very eyes. No one must ever interfere with the right of man to love and love must not be condemned.

Society may laugh at you and judge you a brute, when you lower yourself by bringing out your animal lust for your loved partner. Probably, it is from grudge. However, by that moral thought, comes a more beautiful conception of love and when he puts feelings of real affection first, coupled by union of souls, it culminates (highest climax) in the deepest satisfaction of bodily union with the joy, which words cannot describe but can only felt. So, your vein is flushed with heated blood and your sexual passion arouses? Then, go right ahead and sort out the means to quench your thirst.

Why be at idle, why waste time? Are you asking yourself, how this could be? Then, the answers are in this very book, all you have to do is read on and do what you are told, for within thyself, must deliverance be sought. Therefore, start anew; this book will help you to achieve your creative powers.

Here are two poems; I treasured since I was a teenager. I cannot recall the author. I found them to be valuable. So, I will now pass them to you.

Opportunity # 1 (anonymous)

Master of human destines am I;
Fame, love and fortune on my footsteps wait;
Cities and fields, I walk, I penetrate;
Deserts and seas remote and passing by;
Hovel and Mart and Palace—soon or late;
I knock unbidden once at every gate;
If sleeping, wake—
If feasting—rise before I turn away;
It is the hour of fate;
Ant they, who follow me;
Reach every state;
Mortals desire and conquer every foe
Save death but those who doubt or
Hesitate; condemned to failure;
Penury and woe;
Seek me in vain and useless implore
I answer not, and return no more.

Of course, what is said here has some merit and influence, especially upon those who drop arms and surrender to ill faith. Most people are familiar with this first opportunity and so, face their future life on their past and pre-distinctive concept of feeling everything is lost and there is no more enjoyable and fruitful earthly race which you will encounter and you will have to explore and discover in this your un-avoidable adventure, based on the advice I have disclosed to you.

Be brave; set sail in this most enjoyable and pleasurable ocean of nectar and bliss. Are you not touched and ready to take flight? I can imagine your built-up excitement you now have and to own your treasure, whoever, it may be as quickly as possible. So, let me take leave here, as I pass you to the other valuable pages ahead.

Remember you are not the first or will never be the last and you are not alone on this free market. I am leading you. So, hold on to my hand tightly (this book), so that even if you slip you cannot fall.

Hope for the better, but just do not stop there, look at what this second savior, the kind-hearted opportunity has in store for you especially when you are in confusion and thinks that all odds are against you. Because this book has taken the title "Family Guide", I had to touch on a variety of topics which I felt to be interesting and meet the taste of the various readers, who may find attraction in their appreciative section.

Opportunity # 2 (anonymous)

They do me wrong, who say I come no more;
When once I knock and fail to find you in;
For every day I stand outside your door;
And bid you wake and rise to fight and win;
Wail not for precious chances passed away;
Weep not for golden ages on the wane;
Each night I burn the records of the day;
At sunrise, every soul is born again;
Dost thou behold they lost youth all against?
Dost reel from righteous retribution's blow?
Then, turn from blotted achieves of the past;
And find the future's pages white as snow;
Art thou a mourner? Rouse from thy spell;
Art thou a sinner? Sins may be forgiven;
Each morning gives thee wings to flee from hell;
Each night a star to guide thy feet to heaven;
Laugh like a boy at splendor that has speed;
To vanish joys be blind and deaf and dumb;
My judgments seal the dead past with its dead;
But never blind a moment yet to come;
Though deep in mire, wrong not your hands and weep;
I lend my arm to all who say, "I can";
No shame-faced, out-cast ever sank so deep;
But yet, might rise and be again a man.

This is your compass, use it to find your bearings and chart your course it will pilot you safe to the shores. Because of popular demands, I have brought in this chapter which, is based on a few hints on psychology, and it could be regarded as the warming up of yourself prior to your entry. Please remember, whatever is said in this book not to do, is simply based for our own good. However, love supercedes everything and should they hinder or interrupt the normal loving relationship between the two of you, then, the choice must rest between you both. Surely if you both have confidence in yourselves, going forward should not be difficult.

You have to decide what is best for both of you and if you have to set aside the good advice herein given, then go right ahead according to your opinion. However, any loving and understandable pair will surely stick to my advice herein given, because they will not want to displease and cause pain to each other.

CHAPTER 3

How to Choose By Planet

Astrology: Science of foretelling events by stars, which is based on pure and accurate calculations. It is liken to a school master, who points out the path so it is left to you to choose, either good or the bad, for by then you will have the knowledge, so make sure you select the best.

Some people may accuse you, should you follow the planetary pattern, to choose a partner or to name your child. However, I will not call this system a superstitious belief, as maybe, most critics would do. People born in a society where these things are nurtured, and so the method happened to cause an indisputable impression on the mind. It has developed into a routine custom so that one may do things without meaning or consciousness. Like poles magnetically, repel each other.

Hence, whether you agree or disagree, accept or reject, I think it will make interesting past-time reading and it merely introduced, so as to meet that understanding of various persons, who may be interested in this section of the work. Should you find no interest in it, then you are free to disregard it. Here we go, check carefully. Are you born under or between the following dates?

ARIES	RAM	Rules over the head and face March 21 to April 19
TAURUS	BULL	Rules over the neck April 20 to May 20
GEMINI	TWINS	Rules the arms. May 21 to June 20
CANCER	CRABS	Rules the breasts June 21 to July 21
LEO	LIONS	Rules the hearts July 22 to August 21
LEO	VIRGIN	Rules the bowels August 22 to September 21
VIRGO	BALANCE	Rules the Lions. September 22 to October 22
LIBRA	SCORPION	Rules the privates October 23 to November 21
SAGGITTAURUS	ARCHER	Rules the thighs November 22 to December 22
CAPRICORNS	GOAT	Rules the knees December 23 to January 19
AQUARIUS	WATERMAN	Rules the legs January 20 to February 18
PICSES	FISHES	Rules the feet- February 19 to March 20 19

YOUR BIRTH STONE

JANUARY:	Garnet	FEBRUARY	Amethys
MARCH	Blood	APRIL	Diamonds
MAY	Emerald	JUNE	Pearl
JULY	Ruby	AUGUST	Sardonyx
SEPTEMBER	Sapphire	OCTOBER	Opal
NOVEMBER	Topaz	DECEMBER	Turquoise

Those born under the fortunate signs, that is, on the right side of the human body, tradition has it, that they will be on top of the godly heights of fortune in riches and long in duration. Evil will be to a small degree. That person will have riches in money, power, diverse happiness and a life of pleasure and fortune. On the other hand, those on the left side of the body, falls under the unfortunate sign. They will have much evil fate (more evil than good) or fortune of poverty, alms, craving and wretchedness, woe and but a few years of course, love blinds all of these and "when the boat gone to falls, e khaan turn back". However, too late, too late, will be the loud and unceasing cry with your hands pressing on your aching head without relief from the problems followed by the expressions of several and all kinds of wishes.

Thoughts and wishes are the same. If however, they parted, always look forward with eager expectations to the time, when they will reunite again. True love gives a touch of exquisite pleasure, only to those whose nature harmonizes. A conservative woman and an extravagant or disorderly man will never get along nor could a wasteful woman and a saving man. If they marry their true attraction and being loved and honored, they would always have a chance towards a better existence. A woman's nature is one that deserves true love above all things, followed by sexual satisfaction. She at all times want someone to love her, care honor and provide their finite (boundless) love and for the want of this, she prefers to do without a meal, costly clothes and beautiful jewelry and do not care for wealth. Sometimes, a beautiful flower may bloom and many times fade, wasting its beauty and exquisite fragrances upon the chill passing air. Similarly, young girls and women have grown pale and lonely. Their beauty-forms, fading away in a coffin. Maybe, suicide just because their desires to be loved and honored have not been meaningfully satisfied.

There are too many people today, whose lives are tragedies. They think and rely on their faith and destiny to lead a life of burden and sorrows, believing fate or destiny compels them and so, make no attempt to break the evil spell, but live along with it. These same types of people are the ones who get very accustomed to acceptance of their ready state and make no attempt to change it.

Absolutely, you cannot let your talent, ability, youth and hope dies, only to suffer the consequences all the days of your life. With all the aspiring thoughts I will now proceed to explain more of the astrological signs. There are three signs of the zodiac and to each of them, four elements.

- The positive or head sign—repellent pole.
- The center or equatorial sign—center pole.
- The negative sign—negative attractive poles.

Fire people and water people will not agree because they are natural foes. While fire and air are friends and will agree fine. Fire cannot burn without air; likewise air and earth will agree and at other times be on the warpath. Positive signs will disagree, very strongly and moderately with the center signs.

Positive Pole	Equatorial Pole	Negative Pole
Fire—Aries—fortunate	Leo—fortunate	Sagittarius—fortunate
Earth—Taurus—unfortunate	Virgo—unfortunate	Capricorns—unfortunate
Air—Gemini-fortunate	Libra—ortunate	Aquarius—fortunate
Water—cancer—unfortunate	Scorpio—unfortunate	Pisces—unfortunate

The above is analyzed in more detailed way for your better understanding and less problem in selecting your rightful partner.

I have released a summary of none intricate section on astrology which perhaps will avoid any misunderstanding in this most important field as it applies to love affairs. I have already stated that there are three divisions: positive, equatorial and negative poles, with each carrying four elements as follows in the same order and with their fortunate and unfortunate positions plus they are influenced by fire, air, earth and water.

The positive signs are aggressive, assertive and repellent to each other and part of the time they will also agree and disagree with the middle or equatorial pole.

The equatorial or neutral pole is lucky because people born under it could also agree or disagree with the negative pole.

The negative pole is the receiver and friendly pole as against the positive pole, which is a giver and it is strongly attracted to the negative pole.

Fire signs and air signs agrees well and likewise, earth and water will agree well for these are friendly to one another. Inter-mixture e.g. earth and air will partly agree particular, if air don't go too high for earth as result sometime they will make a paradise and sometime a hell. However air stirs water to greater aims, heights and achievement while fire and water would not agree. Water will out it.

Like signs almost are constant and uniform and they are suitable to one liking as I understand it, except in cases where two heads signs each of it strive to rule the other e.g.: two persons born under the same like planets Aries or other planets.

Thus, if you are an intelligent person and act wisely from what is briefly disclosed to you? It will not be too difficult for you to observe your mistake and to correct your fault and temper so as to be lifted up above the elements. Thereby become equally attractive to all because love, happiness and peace are the greatest concern and desire to both parties. Do not allow your good virtues to be swallowed up in your stubborn haughtiness and rocky faultiness but rather you should try with every effort to be faultless by eating the good fruits of life. If you happen to fall then discard without intentionally hurt anyone and most of all hurting yourself. To overcome faulty problems will cause harmony to be consciously maintained and to the joy of all by this behavior the marriage and or courtship problems and quarrels which always a disgraceful brawl between two lovers could be overcome. Thus be that grand spiritual love partners in physical practice. Remember that love exceeds all barriers except blindness.

Hence some people will continue to seek love and marriage out of the astrological guide. Included herein are the common law of couples and those that elope, it will be observed that they will all go with the love demand regardless of the consequences good or bad. Perhaps since they are already together nothing is wrong with the amends and also nothing is wrong up to that wise point. Some people stroll to their throne like a force rule and behave like a tiger and dies like a dog. He or she is a great barbarity to each other equally as slave to their evil passion as they set their love aside.

For some class of people love seems baffled like a fallen screw from a machine. So at that point it has no value however the same screw has great value when recovered and again go back to your position in your treasure as your attachment of pleasure and enjoyment, which are already there. It is often thought that because of present day civilization combined with increased knowledge of the human race, it is felt that any person could marry who is their heart desire. This allows true love to be the ruler and forgiveness the corner stone plus you do not permit the entry of superiority over one another which is truly among the chief enemy including of gossips, poor-ness and masters to abolish your love. As a result of these no one at this stage is determined to take the slant or bend backward he or she is too proud to put an end to his or her passion which is the destruction element. As a self-test when things get back to normal and you are agreeing back in love just look back and consider your moments of outburst of hasty rage, fury and silly behavior and only then from this examination you will observe how foolish and in ignorance both acted. Experience shows that from weakness and inferiority complex most women will never the first or take the lead to back-down or to be silent.

In nature of this kind, men are presumed to be the leader depending on the culture you grew up in. Hence, you have to take the lead and be the example to be the first to be quiet and let love completely take over as the ruler for both of you. You are its agent so let it be the head of all affairs whether it be right or wrong and my emphasis here in such love is always right and holds the key to solutions in this field.

CHAPTER 4

Love

First you have to see someone, either physically or spiritually (imagination) and then develop your love for that person. Later on, I will give you the vast meaning of love and how it could be practiced for good or evil. This period is of a shying, secret approaches and meetings, not wanting to be exposed so early.

There are several stages or degrees of love, when put into action e.g.

(a) Love towards God.

(b) Love towards kings, country, subjects and countrymen.

(c) Family, relative love; i.e. mother father children brothers, sister's etc.

(d) Passionate love, as husband and wife and lovers. Thus with husband and wife, or lovers there can be broken down into:

    (1) Those that can be experienced in affection that is ordinary or natural love that is equally shared between husband and wife.

    (2) Excessive love, which is transferred into jealousy. These are the two that I wish to deal with and to open the eyes of my readers.

The result of simple, true love could be a mutual happy marriage life or the same love into jealousy put into action would experience great evil of unhappiness, quarrels, hatred, injuries, malice, vindictiveness and even murder. With all of these surface qualities, yet deep down in the heart, there is love for the one who behaves in this manner, for he or she, just cannot do without one another. May I persuade you, not to get involved in this type of love, which will surely ruin both parties' lives.

Love is not a one party business, but rather responsive and it is cooperation from both sides. Hence, a woman will obtain full sexual stimulation and pleasure when she and her partner have equality. Or possibly all matters and the passionate love and union pleasures are mutually shared. Hence, it must be done together, rather for the other person (this is the same thing with each other). A woman will only be sexually equal, when a man accepts that a woman is not merely a sexual receptacle, just for pleasure and fun and also, when the woman accepts that the man is not merely a sexual instrument, on which a love tune is to be played, but rather, equal respect for each other and from each other.

Love for the opposite sex, is seen in the many physically contributing factors such as follows: the clothes we wear, the occupation we serve, relaxation through sports and games, short stories, the way we speak, the tone of voice, the smile and our beauty, manners, courtesy, etiquette, music, art, sculpture, poetry, novels, movies and drama etc, As matter of fact, those contributing factors, constantly reminds us, that man and woman are different from other animals and it is the fundamental instinct which brings a man and a woman together. It is the de-coilable magnet within that heart of the human race. We do not know or yet understand the psychology, other than passing it on to love, which motivates man and woman, boy and girl of hopes, desires, lust and passion.

Sex and love are omnipresent, everywhere and comes building and blinding us from several angles and quite surprisingly, and amazingly. Many intelligent men and women, when facing with these are utterly at a loss and ignorant of the true significance. Some seeking refuge to their nervousness by throwing of only a question themselves after the ordeal, as to their own conduct and maybe, subsequently, feel shame and blame themselves for their failure in a splendid opportunity.

Sex and love, are red-blooded things. They are full with high passion. They live love and fight like giants who instructs or destroy, make or break if it is understood or not. This is a challenge, which man must and gladly accept and not to betray the God-given trust, for man and woman are here on earth for a purpose. So, fulfill it.

Love and understanding go together as hands and gloves. Give too much of one and the other would suffer (jealous) and this is when the marriage would fail. Love is giving to someone a portion of your dearest heart. It is thinking most of the time about he or she, whether that someone is near or far physically however, you cause the one to be always spiritually. You see through imagination and thoughts and send messages on the wings of the winds and this is telepathy (action of one's mind on another at a distance). Love, is sharing good or bad as though it is part of you, on this count, however, a good husband will not want to burden a loving wife, she would feel left out and un-cared for. Then she would become the problem child. So with good sense and reasoning, you will have to take care of the situation, as condition warrants.

Love is feeling tenderness, caring and show concern about the smallest things e.g. a little touch, and un-painful pinch, squeeze or bite, a kiss at random anywhere and small gifts now and then. It is caring when there is sadness or illness. Love is glowing in the warmth that special moment brings and it is finding happiness in the first touch or smiles follows by the wink and cut-eye (a stared glance). It is everything that counts. It is what matters and makes life worth-while going for an adventure.

In many societies where women are less exposed or in the nude, the breast is a powerful unparalleled sexual symbolism and is a powerful attraction, for the male's eyes. The communities, in which she lives, and was, brought up, do have an impact on her action, attitudes, behaviors and customs. All parts that constantly covered with clothing have a different complexion, and as soon as these, are exposed to the eye of the man, his passion of love and sexual desires are aroused.

I said earlier, that lovemaking involves a lot of childish and seemingly foolish manipulations, petting and foreplay for sexual intercourse to be truly enjoyed and have the well-meant desired results. Let's look at the medical doctors for example, who is in gloves most of the time, due to their hygienic knowledge, they would hardly indulge in much kissing, cuddling and foreplay with their wife, because of his professional background and would regard much of it as unclean. The female doctor can hardly explain the pleasures of oral sex, although she may long to do the experiment. Likewise her husband, especially if he is also a doctor and as an upper professional, would not entertain such an act and no doubt, she will be afraid to introduce such an enjoyable request.

Social diseases could be the reason to abstain and precaution is a good fencing, but this greets all class of people, where or when it is existing. The male doctor gets opportunities to flirt around and do have girlfriends. However it is a disadvantage to the female doctor who, rarely have the opportunity to an outsider. Let it be known that there are honest and dishonest people in every walk of life and it penetrates in every class of the human race.

Perhaps, to the shallow minded person of which surely there must be a few in society at all times, the thought may be why worry over the presentation of such a book on that type of subject. Of course, whether we read from a book or not by virtue of nature and society all of us somehow, or the other will get involve in love affairs, coupled by its agencies and or by products.

As a result, such type of person would be dis-interested and pay no attention to develop any further knowledge along this line. However, my book varies and covers a wide range on family matters of great interest and so you are sure to meet with matters and information's you no doubt, already know about, inclusive of many important matters that bound to catch your attraction and admiration. So, at least that part will be useful to you.

There are also other persons, who might be too busy or in a hurry and well overtaken, so they will pay less attention to a book of this kind. They will not find or set aside any time to read what is regarded as the most important bliss in life which, words cannot really explain.

It is the beginning of life—how, where and why life begins and is responsible for the existence of all of us. Without this relationship, be it natural or artificial, there would be no life increase or multiplication in all the various types of population on land, air and water and for sure, it is GOD'S law.

This business might have you busy and be time consuming that very little time is left over for one another. As a result, those that are sincere feels loss of the true impact in its togetherness, so quite a lot in this field is half done, too hurriedly done inclusive that very often none is even done at all.

No doubt, all of you are right in your action chosen, because if the freedom of thought which is so often placed and applied wrongly. May I remind you that wherever there is right, there is wrong and wherever there is wrong, right is also the over-looker. So, without right—wrong will not be known. Hence, it is suggested that whoever, or whatever you are, please place both on the scale and examine the case and its cause well before you do place it in your opinion box of guilty, because out there are plenty around and without you tasting them, you will never know from experience how good they are. This does not refer to sexual intercourse rather the many other contacts and reasoning by which opinions are to be extracted from.

When you find your enjoyment, you may no doubt want to or even start to blame yourself for your late push venture. This book is about all and more of this and do take care of them so that you shall have no regrets whatsoever. Here is a little clear-out and dry hint for you to follow. Most men are better lovers, when they pay attention to the things that are important to a woman, such as getting her excited while being gently. She takes notice of your every love action and expressions admirably while she appreciates to be admired. You never think of it just let a woman loose in the bedroom red-hot and she becomes a new person from her temper of love and desire of fulfillment. She turns into a wild sexual animal, having dropped all her emotional shame and replaces it by the enjoyment of sexual pleasure.

When the desire is on for sexual intercourse, the woman love to go to bed with her husband and of course there is no feeling in the whole wide world as exquisite and exciting from a husband when you desire him and having him take possession of you. When, surely the moment of expectation grows with the then gradual increasing tension as he approaches you with the searing (hot erect penis) stab of entry and finally the explosion in the vagina by both lovers.

From experience, no doubt science may have discovered it also, that it is true that women do have more sexual stamina than men, for they do not need recovery period after an orgasm also one orgasm even two organisms don't usually make them fell like turning over to sleep. They could have successive orgasm, they are multi-organic as against a husband, whose erection falls after ejaculation and will take some time before another erection to follow.

It was revealed by some women, that most of them feel that oral sex really turn them on and that they may like it, and sometimes prefers it being done to them without being asked for. They look forward to it as a natural course of lovemaking and it sometimes may feel better than penis insertion.

Two ways sex and even three ways such as anal, oral vagina and breast sucking inclusive of foreplay have mentioned elsewhere in this book not for practice but for knowledge. It must not be misunderstood nor misinterpreted because you are the one who have the physical role or performance in this love journey. This book is therefore to be treated as a guide, a brother or friend and lover's servant to all whose hearts is grieved, sore and heavy-laden while travelling life's strange paths. The outcome of which is a real great home for humanity.

Marriage is called the sliver link that binds two strange or even relative hearts together. It is known from the earliest ages, the institution of matrimony has cherished the holiest and best of human institutions and intelligence. The wisest and purest in all times have been its most strenuous advocate. In this scared and appreciable association, the painter and the poet have found alike equally their highest vision of beauty and as well the orator and essayist a theme most potent in its appertains of eloquence (most powerful use of language).

History has chosen that in all ages of the world, as I have read that those who have married are truly given that silver link. This silken thread by its scared knot binds two honest and willing, hearts to the everlasting joy. It is the two lutes turning in one key and two melting and longing hearts into one. Time seems to separate for too long. It's the blending of nature's beauty of the lily (man) with the roses (woman) and the natural earthly fragrance with a more heavenly constituency of our unblemished nature. It is a heaven on earth life's paradise, not forgetting it's the soul's earthly quest, earth's immortality and as an eternity of pleasure.

Marriage that is lost in the night of time shows man's joy is increased and his sorrows lessened. It wisely doubles the joys and pleasure and divide the grief of earthly existence. Marriage was given to man and woman for their highest good as it is said that man was made for God's pleasure and glory, hence the very inheritance for the woman and the woman for the man. It is the sweetest and purest most earnest and heavenly of earthly happiness and is found in the sacred enjoyments in the home circle and should not be in adultery.

There is none so bad or discarded that true and loving marriage may not redeem, none so bright, pure and good that it will not make brighter, purer and better still as long as holy or loveliness remain on earth. Love, will be the last footprints in the stony heart of the last home, depraved and their last association will be with the sacred characters of husband and wife.

The excitement at the commencement of lovemaking is indeed marvelous and thrilling to the young couple. Some women with steamily erotic adventures as she cares, drops the succulent (juicy sound of love) ravishing (sweep or carry away) take you intimately through her torrid sex life sultry (hot and close) undress you to a point of excitement that you rarely attain in real bed.

Thus, taken in consideration, the women especially those in need are always communicating sexually. Even if you don't have intercourse, for when she walks down the street and a man looks at her opened or exposed breast or almost thinly or partly exposed body as modern customs are or the exposed upper part of the legs isn't she communicating her desire to him?

Your deepest satisfaction in owning the grand volume on this subject is the surety that what you do not know possibly lies between its covers to be reached easily at your convenience, whenever you are ready to master thus wonderful art.

As a beginner let it clearly known that nothing that is, anything which appears to you to be hidden is lost but at the same time nothing that is found is absolutely new as perhaps is the opinion of man. Again, that the seal of eternity (everlasting love) is affixed in the soul of all both men and women by good nature to that truth which is the reflection of its glory of which words are insufficient to describe.

Thus, for you to obtain favor and love of the opposite sex may appear difficult or perhaps impossible, having filled with fear and doubts. However, the processes for obtaining such a mysterious favor and devoted love will truly be the experiments and directions from both the opposite sex with either one, more often the male as set forth in this work which makes it's a valuable book. Understand it clearly no matter how prudent one maybe the wonderful information given will always arouse the love passion and force you to one another as do magnet.

The greatest charm of exquisite existence and success is personal satisfaction that is to know and realize that your hearts desires and wishes be it what it maybe are being fulfilled on target and is also satisfied within expectations. They must not be tampered with prolonged over dire impatience and frustration all of which breeds contempt. Too many young people today whose loves are tragedies filled with burden and sorrows reap the reward of a broken heart. These are miseries, which follow you like the shadow follows the ox that draws the plough.

You should not smother your talent nor trample your ideas and allow your ability such as youth or even the elderly and dearest hopes to be shattered or die. And as a consequence suffer all the days of your remaining life just for the want of a little effort and courage on your part which is truly standing nearby your side and is ready to give you all the support without fail. As it stands there it is silently telling you that you will receive the fullest and it's all at such an important time. Everyone is heir to all the virtues and faults plus success and failures equally in this world. As customary the weaker character does not very often struggle nor even take a step further to up a fight in order to gain success. On the other hand the brave and strong character never sits hopelessly. They are the ones that see winning as something worth fighting for and would make sure they fight to the end.

It will prove to be a good companion and never failing one as you come to realize that opportunities and possibilities are all simple and at your fingertips which otherwise may not have been known. It gives you here, a lot of wonderful knowledge of both the good and the bad on love matters including other essentials that are attached in this field.

This book, I can assure you will prove that the cheapest or otherwise less the will that produces tragic consequences, advisable therefore, you are to have control over your negative and disturbing emotions and go forward to your love one at the proper moment.

Thus, when I referred to sexual starvation, elsewhere in this book, I did not intend to limit this to just the sexual intercourse only, which covers the types of foreplay and manipulations before the sex act and after the sex act.

Too often, it may happen by very few lucky lovers, who will fulfill all these simple but very important four stages, which are very appreciative and are desired by almost every female in particular. She will not disclose it to you, because you did not train her to do so and although, she suppresses the desires, if you are a good love-maker and observer, you will see it in her and felt it in her body.

As mentioned above, some lovers (husband) may fulfill one step and that is foreplay while he will be hopeless failure or don't bother with the two other stages. He will be late for the flight, so he will go after a hurry half-done job by going to the female right away. This will bring out very little enjoyment and so, a job is being done just for doing it sake.

Some people may be very romantic and do a very good job during the actual sex act, by fulfilling her desire in every way in this stage, but lacks the two other stages that is before and after the act. He will be just on and off and finish at that. Again, it appears as if he was in a hurry to catch the express train. This is bad; he is too late and is in a hurry in everything when it comes to all the requirements in love making.

Some people will be very good at and before and during the sexual acts with all the desired romantic indulgences, but after he gets what he had wanted and found gold, he strikes it rich and cares no further. He then turns his back against the wife, becomes drunk as it were, and is in a hurry wither to sleep or to complete the other unfinished work. He is on the warpath, until he again is ready to make use of the using tool, for sexual purposes.

The best persons, are those who would have fulfilled all the romantic, lovemaking practices to their partners, during that period which is supposed to be the most important than all other things, for that moment and to themselves. They would take their time to do what is to be done and they would express their enjoyment of the flesh, which will have a pleasing psychological effect on the woman. You are to concentrate on what you are doing and what to do. Enjoyment must be your goal in lovemaking, which goes with the over all-sexual acts.

My thoughts quite recently were preoccupied with these two powerful extreme groups, where one set of people may be starving and the other set may be having abundantly. If you happen to fall in the groups of abundance then I must say do enjoy and make the most of it because the beauty of the taste won't last forever

Now that you know better it is not too late to use your knowledge wisely. More than likely you will be saving the pieces from falling apart. Give it your best and see it create that path for you. Our stay on earth is short and without extravagance, over indulgence and damages to yourself, make this stay an enjoyable and fruitful one. There should be no regrets. Eat wear and act moderately. It is said that the one that knows better must do better at all times. So, because he or she submits him or herself first, for an amicable settlement for love and peace, this action very often is misconstrued, for weakness by the other party, who still boastfully acts in passion lies in the bossoms of fools. However for the purpose of peace, the stronger is knowledge, becomes the weakest for the satisfactorily agreement, which is so necessary if a marriages to last.

To meet the challenges ahead safely and to enjoy the adventure of the sweet and mysterious wonder, man should become thoroughly acquainted and familiar with the manual that you own, (habits and desires) before he gets sexually involves with the woman he passionately loves. When service is required, remember, you know your partner/wife/lover best, and you do have the necessary required mechanical skills and tools to do the make-up that lies ahead.

CHAPTER 5

Court-Ship

Having fall in love, communications will start. This is the period when you will meet as often as possible, maybe, even go out of your way to see and meet each other. Boldness start to increase and you act partly in secret and partly in the open; with little concern should your actions be known. It is during this stage promises are made and planning for marriage life, children bearing, caring and how to manage the remainder of life for the future, it is however, true that many promises made are not kept or fulfilled, for one reason or another because they were not genuinely made but came out from excitement, anxiety and in ignorance they were made.

Both lovers are guilty promise breakers. I must remind you that choosing a partner are a lifetime venture of togetherness; it is like gambling for the future. So you are to be sober minded, level minded and not to be carried away by emotional ideas and flattery. You need to apply intelligence of your sensitive storehouse (brain).

In this period, this is really a planning stage and getting to know each other. You are to touch as wide a field as possible and clear the air on differences of opinions, so that after marriage, there is one unified thought into the stepping stone of love, where you may approach things that would arise throughout life's journey.

By freely conversing with each other, you are to study from disclosures, the likes and dislike of each other, with a view to implement the acceptable ones through life's journey. As the good old sayings "a good woman" is hard to find, so depending on what this may mean, for I see two sides in it. However, it is clear, that there are good women. Hence, seek and you shall find.

That is, "you meet her good" as the saying goes. However, absence of the hymen of a women does not necessarily mean that she is not good or that she had sexual intercourse before (this good also refer to the ways, habits and customs of the woman and her virginity). She could very well be a virgin, for there are many ways whereby the hymen could be punctured or get damaged, due to no direct fault of the young woman, on the other hand, there are cases of young women having sexual intercourse or fulfillment and her hymen are still intact, hence, she will be called a virgin or a maiden girl. While in true fact, she is not, because she had sexual intercourse.

The possibility of this truth is as follows: the young woman while having sexual intercourse there was no penetration of the penis into the inner part of the vaginal passage. However, with the penis and movements coming in contact with the clitoris, this will cause the climax and an orgasm. Thus fulfillment of all desires of natural intercourse, for the male semen will also flow or ejaculate and both parties will get their full satisfaction or orgasm. Just as if there was a penetration in the vagina (orgasm, is the climax which the highest pitch of sexual excitement) and at this point, the sensation triggers the ejaculation of the semen from the male sex organs.

The female orgasm is a more generalized feeling of sexual satisfaction and release of tension. It is not necessary for a woman to have orgasm to become pregnant.

While courting, you as a prospective mate should check on the following:-

1. That the expected partner should come from a reasonable good family background that is also free of serious hereditary defect.
2. The matter of health of the individual in important.
3. Similarity of interest and cultural background.
4. Ability to show what should be done in a given set of circumstances or situation, such as how when and where and why it is to be done.

5. Knowledge as to how the individual behaves with friends and treat members of their family and how the individual is regarded by his or her own or other members of the opposite sex.
6. Each party must understand the attitude of each other towards children, sex and morality.
7. Look into the suitability of body, shape, height, odor etc.
8. Look into financial ability
9. Courtship should be long enough to give a better knowledge and understanding of the individual.
10. Above all, love for each other must be the same and sure and not doubtful, thus making the sure requirements sacrifices for each other and prefer him or her (as love ones above all others).

I am sure, on many occasions of husbands and wives misunderstanding you would have heard the many unpleasant, however, not meaningful remarks hurled at each other. The woman may have said to their husbands, "Oh, why did I ever marry you? I could have done better!" followed by other unkind words and regrets from the other. Many men have said to their wives, "well, you were determined to have me, so now you must make the best of me". On most occasions, none of these remarks are true and meaningful and no doubt, without foundations because they arouse from hasty conclusions.

To avoid, or at least to minimize the above after problems. It is the suitor—the man who is to ask the girl's parents or guardians, consent for her hand in marriage. So during this courtship at some point not too early, he will propose—that is put the question of marriage to her and with her approval, the man must now approach the father for the hand of his daughter in marriage. At such meeting, some of the things to discuss of which the father will be interested to learn from you, as an honorable man of which you should state: your income and source of it; your future prospects; or what you should settle for.

Family history, your personal character and history, plus such things that the prospective father-in-law wishes to know before he could fully decide to exchange his daughter's parental happiness into the care of another person. Who, up to the time, a stranger and is little known.

All things being equal and you are accepted, then wedding arrangements will be gone into and maybe fashioned as per financial resources, coupled with custom of the day and religious background.

Engagement is the forerunner of the wedding. After this is done, movements between the intended are to be limited, particularly alone in private visits to parents or relatives by either parties. Dressings should be moderate. The girl should not attend functions alone. The outcome of these things could be very distasteful, if these advises are overlooked.

Avoid harmful mistakes of newlyweds and other married couples because this book has ideal sex techniques and methods for satisfactory sex acts. You are to keep a sharp eye out at this courtship period and it is not too hard for you to remember that some "white face hairy black heart and pass eye does grow". You do not have to be hasty, rough or brutal manner, but in a very cool headed and tasteful way. By this crucial time and you will have the golden opportunity to ride the "high way in a train, which leads to progress in love and marriage.

It is true; school life is responsible for the beginning of many love affairs, although truly, many of these lovers do not have the opportunity to be husband and wife. Because after this period, they get separated, going in different direction and when they happen to see each other again, it is too late. Of course, many of this love are not really true love but merely appreciation and are too young and ignorant for a deep-seated love, and often they do not even know the meaning or significance of passionate love. Theirs are undoubtedly, a routine custom of being together and so they cannot really account.

A beautiful girl, well adored and dressed with fine jewelry, will pose a picture of such dazzling beauty, that a "fire eye man" will be swept clean off his feet and may think, to delay, is dangerous pursue he could lose her to someone else. Of course, such type of girl, before you realize it, you will have competition and the fittest may survive. So, you will have to act there and then because you do not want to lose this splendid doll.

Boy, "when man tek wife, e gat fo tie e wais string, oh, man neva tink money too much fo spen", if you understand courtship to be the period of influence, discussion and wooing your lover to your side, then does courtship ever ends? The answer is, a blunt NO! Because even after marriage, this behavior of wooing each other over his or her side continues and this would never cease. You will agree, and this is how it should really be. But it must be done in a loving way, with surprise kiss now and then.

The wife, whose mouth could cut iron, tries to get the husband who is less talkative, to her side of a dispute. So, do the husband who is less argumentative towards the wife. Here, both of you disagree to agree. The sun must not go down with any remaining wrought between the two of you. Nothing must be so large that there cannot be forgiveness and a loving make-up between both of you very promptly.

It is said, since in time of old, "true love never dies", regardless of the problems, complications and persecutions that may show up between the two lovers from time to time. On many occasions, many men put the wrong foot forward, rather than to think well and start their conversation in the right direction and moreover, to be true and well-meant intentions. Some men are as I said, before unsettled, bashful, nervous, excited, fearful and shy. What is surprising about most of these young men is that when they are with their friends, they are put to the test by their boastful and chatty with lots of mouth friends.

Courtship should last for not more than a year, or within a year. The lovers should be in a position to arrive at an amicable conclusion. This is however discretionary and the lovers could decide earlier that is, anytime within a year. Leading up to their marriage.

Most young men press on for sexual intercourse before marriage that are, between the courtship and engagement period, which is commonly known as the probation period. Any man, in my opinion, with this attitude, is untrained and undisciplined, and most occasions, selfish and cannot be trusted, because after getting what he wanted, he leaves the girl with a broken heart and sometimes use the incident as a curse and blackmail upon her. There are however, still some honest men who, will stick to their love promises and marry. Whether, they interfere with the girl sexually or not.

Of course, this is truly a trying and difficult period for the young girl. In going through the test and to still hold her lover, when will have to be very wise and act in a sensible manner when confronted with these class of men, who ties to force pre-marriage sexual intercourse.

To give into pre-marriage sexual intercourse, might destroy the girl's character by the ill conceive minded man, who may be just a "hit and run" person and had been all the way pretending to love her. If, on the other hand, she did not give in to his request for pre-marriage sexual intercourse, then she may lose him to some other girl, who may entice him away by fulfilling his pre-marriage sexual desires.

The test is now confusion switched on a young mind. What the girl is to do in such a situation? Nothing more but is to stand firm and "NO" is to be the answer in a polite way. After all, the girl is not a "market fish" on sale or for a gift or for a sample, that anyone could take a taste.

Beware, for your own good. If you fail to agree and he truly loves you, then you denying him intercourse before marriage will have no adverse effect between the love for you. This is where you win the game.

Should he be dis-satisfied with your stand of a courteous NO, and he wishes to bring the love affairs to an end, then let it be at this early stage, where your grief will be but short and less painful or severe.

"Love is blind" after all, this saying is true, only when it is properly, rightly and un-pretensively applied—remember again "true love never dies" for the sincere person, but the hit and run or pretend ones "love do die" a miserable death and should be forgotten forever.

During this period of courtship, correspondence are usually accompanied with small gifts now and again as a token of appreciation but most of all attractive and weighty love verses are enclosed to express your various degrees of affection for the lover. Could this ocean of wonderful love be "till death do us part?" If so, the marriage would always be a happy one and you will never want to be out of sight of each other, even for a short moment and this will surely be, if both parties adhere to the advice given in this book, which is totally prepared to achieve this purpose.

Before I leave this chapter, I wish for you to consider this story. A loving mother gearing for the customary Christmas, along the usual tradition, called her son and sent him to purchase currants and prunes, but on his way to the shop, he forgot the flavoring ingredients for the cake. After a hard thinking, tar, oakum and pitch came to his mind and so, he purchased them and took these wrong items home but of course, those could not have been used for the cake but on a leaking ship, which was not present.

Take heed, therefore, for when you think you are on the right course, you may rather be on the wrong. Do not purchase (choose) the wrong lover, less you will be unevenly yoked; so for help and guide, why not turn to the section of this book which deals with "how to choose by planet".

Ancient people were guided and the Hindus used it and there were less broken homes and although the system is still being used by these people in these modern days, there are a very larger number of broken homes. Why is it so? You may ask. Well, the responsible person, who is to check on the planetary agreement purposely misguide the lovers and give them false information's that their planets agree. So, they can go ahead and marry just because he do not want to break up the love affairs of the two lovers, by telling them the truth it will be seen, that mostly not the system is wrong but the false person that used the system for money. Parents on the other hand will only consent, seeing the determination of the lovers from mere frustration, in such type or evenly matched love, simply to avoid a calamity or unfortunate problems which will result in shame and disgrace to the entire family.

This battle for pre-marital sexual intercourse, is also used by some smart men to test their lovers—the common saying here is "me mek a ting to see if me a gu ketch a ting". In other words, they were first testing the girls and if they give in, then, the men would regard them as "bad girls" and that they would give-in to pre-marriage sexual intercourse to any person who is courting them, and so, they are unsafe to make a decent and trusted wife. As a result, the men would fulfill their desires and never to be seen again. If you are a cake then you need currants, raisins and prunes, but if you are a leaking ship, then you will need tar, oakum and pitch and when the fox cannot get the grape he said that "it is sour".

Courtship Between A cockerel an a Pullet

What has been depicted in this chapter is now summarized in this wonderful story, which you may not have heard before. I happen to find it very interesting that is why I will pass it on to you.

One day, a pullet (young hen) was scratching and feeding in the yard. She was beautiful and displayed her beauty with a measure of haughtiness, while she went along graciously in the yard. A cockerel (young cock) that was nearby, gazed upon her, became attracted and so, without any further ado, he approached in his cool splendor, to make love to the hen. He went, with a leaping on one side, spread down his one side wing and with a slight increase in movements and a dignified semi-circle in front of the hen, he said to her "I L-O-V-E Y-O-U", but the hen, although interested at first sight of the cockerel, pretended she did not hear what he said and so continued to pick up feed on the ground. Quickly, the smart cockerel, showed no annoyance, but thought up another plan and so with the same charming action, he turned around and returned in a semi-circle almost touching her, this time so she bound to take notice and he said to her this time—"I got an account that worth millions of dollars with a reputable bank and before the hen could have replied he turned back and repeat in the same fashion and said to her "you can have it all" this was too much for her, at this point, she was caught with the flattering promises and as she could have resisted, she just sit down and said to the cock, :take what you want"—thus they both made love (had intercourse). After that the cock with the same semi-circle, outstretched wing downward and politeness said to her "did you enjoy yourself?'. But, the hen just turned aside and was silent.

The old saying is "fire one wait for the result", some weeks later, the hen went to lay and she went through a lot of pain and strain before the egg was laid. An ordeal, she will never forget. So, there after she came out terrible annoyed with abusive words, hurled to the nearby to find the cock but the cock had no time for her. He simply flew up a nearby fence, flapped his wings and crowed in merriment, as thought he was tantalizing the hen. The elderly people knows, that this is exactly what transpires when two young person's meet and at courtship time.

Have you learnt a lesson from this story? There are many questions that will trigger the outcome going in different directions. So in the future, pay more attention when you see a cock and hen around, listen to their discourse and what transpires and you will find it as described in this story.

Truly marriage used to be called a lottery, but today, it is in most cases, pronounced a failure. In a lottery you either win, lose or draw at the game. If you enjoy the happiness of marriage for what is intend for then you have won the lottery, and if per chance misfortune (divorce) then you have lost in your gamble. It is truly a mystery of magnetic and repulsion forces, however whether bad or good, LOVE and marriage legally or illegally will continue to the end of time. To be fair to you, I must disclose to you that some marriage problems will be solved, while some will remain unsolved; however if Love had its way coupled with forgiveness, then these could be regarded as solved.

Do you need help? Then take it from the helper, because the person, who does not investigate, often denies the facts or truth of anything. The knowledge advanced in this course, as contained, in this volume treats on several branches and lead the enthusiastic student to higher places of successful thoughts as well as showing the adventurer, the deeper mysteries in this everlasting and true; light of the path of love and its attribute. The nectar of love illuminates the secret wisdom and zealous desires. Thus the beginner is enabled to intelligently with consciousness take the first step on the existing path. The once silent voice will now excel and proceed as a storm of LOVE, anxiety in action, which will no longer be a secret, but real matter and force out if the once sleeping mind. You will easily win friendship and the hearty co-operation of others instead of arousing resentment, friction or resistance. The knowledge, which applies to you through these chapters, is not relationship to fortune telling or superstition, but should be in good fate taken as a doctor's advice. The teachings bear a message of Love, hope, for the lost lover, and the conquest of self. The evil you do lives after you, but the very evil goes and reach the destination before you, as it becomes a leader. Out of evil cometh good. So let your aspiration be fully in this direction.

CHAPTER 6

Kisses

Earlier, I told you of classified kisses. I will now explain the meaning of kisses, because you may have seen people indulged in kissing each other in various ways, which may have aroused your curiosity and may very often use it as slander against the individual. But, did you ever stop and give it a thought as to what each may signify in a social civilized society? I think, it is therefore fitting for me to up-date you in this field, where you can find eight ways which are in practice over many years to the present time and it is good for you to know of them, so whenever you may happen to see them in use, you may not be like others who misunderstand what they have seen and to go away with the wrong idea.

Kisses, like flowers, are used to express the feelings of people for one another.

1 Kiss on the lips, this means affection and it also takes care of passionate love.
2 Kiss on the cheek; this denotes respect or salutation.
3 General kissing is a symbol of charity, especially in the early church.
4 Kiss on the beard; means respect to the aged or authority.
5 Kiss on the forehead; means condescension that is to be gracious, patronize, stoop, design.
6 Kiss on the back or palm of the hand, denotes submission and so it is to kiss the feet.

7   To kiss the ground near a person is a mark of respect.

8   To kiss the hand of an idol means worship.

Kissing and caressing goes together and these arouse more exciting thrill, pleasure and enjoyment to the modern lover's as against the far back in the earlier days. Love and romancing carry the popular action of kissing, cuddling and sucking each other tongue and elsewhere as you desire etc. for these indulgence stimulates the long memorable passionate emotion of love as a result therefore none of these could rightly be omitted during love scenery.

To kiss means to caress wittingly, touch or express with both lovers lips and sucking the tongue all of which are passionate system practiced in the art of kissing and which acts of affection, desire, greetings and the true degree of expression etc. and it is the token of sincere love, confidence, trust and manifestation of peace and no ill will but courtesy and respect.

It is evidently clear that the embrace of kissing brings to light the longing desire of appreciation and affection which are no longer a shadow of darkness. It is a caress with the lips of both lovers mouth to mouth and sucking of each other tongue and it is the system being express based on the foundation of love and if the foundation is weak the whole structure will collapse no matter how strong is the super structure.

CHAPTER 7

Flowers

I referred to flowers in a few areas of my work, so it would be unfair not to give you the balance. I am sure it will find a place in your heart, especially because flowers play an important part in lovemaking. It touches the admiration of every woman and if a woman does not take to admire flowers, then, she knows nothing of love and would never be a good lover or a loving wife. The poet, says that flowers were put into the world to beautify the earth and to minister delight to man.

Practically, flowers in arrangement have three sprays of graduated height and have relation to man and the universe e.g. the tall spray represents heaven the second—man and the lowest—earth. These three sprang are sometimes designated by some people—father, mother, and child. They form decoration in homes and in every walk of life. Flowers are used as a symbolic language and code and this was very common long ago in the Orient. One could express his or her thoughts and feelings by means of flowers, which are being sent to someone. According to the occasion e.g. the Lilly denotes innocence, red rose indirectly says I love you; and the white rose—I will marry you. For-get-me-not means friendship.

Following, is a flower list of more detailed explanation. Type of flower and what it means sending or giving to another person.

Amaranth:	Immorality retaining its freshness for a long period of time.
Anemone:	Forsaken
Apple blossom:	Admiration
Aspen leaf:	Fear
Alyssum:	Protection
Basil:	Girl desire, truth, good luck
Burberry:	Protection
Brier:	Insult
Buttercup:	Childishness.
Camellia:	Good luck and nobility of reasoning, expression of devotion.
Calla:	Pride
Candy-tuff:	Indifference
Clover-5 leaves:	Bad luck
Clover-4 leaves:	Good luck
Cornflower:	Heaven, delicacy
Cowslip:	Youthful, beauty
Cypress:	Death
Crocus:	Attachment, cheerful.

Daffodil: Un-requited love.

Daisy: Simplicity, purity and innocence.

Dandelion: Desire, love me, or affection
retuned.

Everlasting: Undying affection

Evergreen: Hope

Eye-bright: Rheumatism

Fern: Confidence, a secret bond of love,
shelter.

Faxglove: Insincerity

Golden rod: Encouragement, treasure and good fortune.

Hellebore: Swelling

Heather: Loneliness and beauty.

Helitrope: Devotion

Hepatica: Anger

Henbone: Fits

Honey suckle: Fidelity

Hyacinth: Playful joy, jealousy.

Ivy: Trust, fidelity, affection.

Lilac: Fastidiousness, beauty, pride and innocence.

Lotus:	Forgetfulness and estrange love.
Laurel:	Victory (fame)
Marigold:	Contempt, cruelty, grief.
Myrtle:	Wedded bliss
Musk rose:	Purity
Monkshood:	Fever
Moss or dry twigs:	Old age
Narcissus:	Vanity, egotism
Nightshade:	Ghost
Oak-leaf:	Power
Orange blossom:	Marriage, eternal love,
Oxalis:	Pangs of regret
Pansy:	Loving thoughts
Palm leaf:	Conquest
Passion flower:	Love and romance, fate.
Primrose:	I cannot live without you, evening, inconstancy.
Red roses:	Passion and remembrance.
Radish flower:	Protection
Rose (yellow):	Infidelity and jealousy

Rue:	Repentance
Rosemary:	Remembrance, loyality.
Scarlet geranium:	A kiss
Snow drop:	A friend in need
Tuberose:	Bereavement, dangerous pleasures.
Tulip:	Boldness
Twig (dried):	Old age
Violet:	Modesty and faithfulness.
Zinnia:	Daily or constant remembrance.

If anyone should send you any of the above flowers, it would mean that he or she is wishing you the effects or telling you of something of their-self. For example, the flower apple blossom, if sent to you by your lover, her or she is telling you that he/she loves or admires you. Scarlet Geranium means the lover wants a kiss and yellow roses means that the lover is jealous of you. If a fern is sent, it means there is secret bond of love. So, you see, flowers do speak a code of language and bring out a significant meaning to you. If the name of the flower is sent it will mean the same thing as if the flower is sent.

Flowers both in color and fragrance hold well in attraction and they convey to all human un-estimated charm and delight peace of mind ever since in the ancient time down to this modern days. Their popularity will never grow old and to date to make the usual love and admiration impact for who can ever say that they don't love flowers.

On the wedding garland of brightly chosen beautiful flowers grace the bridegrooms neck to show love appreciation and acceptance while equally attractive bouquet as present of affection welcome the beautiful and charming bride who is rightly queen of the day.

CHAPTER 8

Engagement

"Love rules the court, the camp, the grove and man
below and saints above for love is heaven and
heaven is love"

W e are accustomed to hear people speak of engagement
to a woman or man and this would mean the forerunner
of the marriage. The more appropriate word to use
which is somewhat more specific is Betrothal, and this precedes the
marriage rite and is a binding engagement—the meaning of betroth
is: a contract to any one in order to marriage.; to promise or pledge
in marriage. This is therefore binding as the marriage itself and is
very often regarded as the first marriage.

To this exercise, there is no definite or laid down formalities. It
may vary according to your choice and religious faith. In general
certain common principles are involved whereby, you may proceed
by inviting friend and family; dress and dressings as you desire;
up-keep entertainment and music may be to your likeness. All of
which is to be at your convenience.

It is the man's responsibility to discuss the desire to engage the
woman and so the woman is being engaged to the man. It is said,
that the woman is made for the man and not the man for the woman.
Maybe, meaning the man was first created and then the woman as
help mate. But where my book is concerned, the woman is made
for the man and similarly, the man is made for the woman. Both

parties belong to each other, for the man is no more for himself nor the woman, but both have equal rights on each other.

All things being set, choice being made and settled, the man will arrive at the girl's home with the engagement ring which is preferable of gold with either diamond, ruby or sapphire embedded thereon. It is wise to consult the girl, what she would appreciate because some girls may prefer their birthstone on the ring.

These are moments of surprises and you will take this first opportunity to give of your best which is a sign of how sincere you love her, coupled with your honesty, loyalty and faithfulness. So, you will have to be tactful, in dealing with her and make her tell you what she would appreciate, although, she is not to be conscious that she had really told you anything. She must not see the ring before and if she insists, then to please her just show her another one and when the right one is produced, the surprise will emotionally over-take her and she will have no time to be annoyed that you were making fun of her.

Having gathered together the religious minister's priest will conduct the engagement ritual and will announce the purpose of the get together. At this point religious beliefs will be initiated accordingly. Engagement ring will be blessed and then the man will placed the ring on the third finger of the left hand. You may give her any other gift as you so desire.

The religious minister (according to your religion) as usual will offer his advice to the couple and speeches may also follow from other guests. The woman will then cut the cake while the man will stick the cake just as it is being done on the wedding day. Other friend in attendance may also give presents to the girl.

While it is not compulsory, it is a common practice for the girl to present the man a ring under the above rituals. After the ceremony, a party of drinks, food and maybe dancing if desired may follow.

Broken Engagement

In the case of a broker engagement, it is the responsibility of both parties and both side parents to maintain and reserve in speech in speech and dignity, refraining from bitter re-criminations that is, to make counter charges or accusations.

The mother is the person, who should make known the fact that the engagement has been broken off but of course, no reason must be offered and the engagement ring, presents and letters should be returned as early as convenient to the donors, with a brief respectable note of explanation and with the avoidance of any impolite expression. A high source of discipline with great caution is needed at this tedious point of time.

Some decent couples do not look back for the return of the engagement gifts and to feel somewhat ashamed to ask for the return of the gifts. They act as if nothing had happened.

As I said earlier, whenever a breaking up and the cause of parting between loved ones present itself. It is indeed a striking blow and effective sadness reveals to them, which upset either party's mind for a long time.

In summary, this is what it is . . . it was better that we never loved so kindly and had never loved so blindly. Had we never met, then we never would have parted. Thereafter, to follow by pain from both of us, the broken hearted and would never to have the cause to bid a sad farewell.

CHAPTER 9

Marriage

As it is in the biblical scripture Heb. 13:4 says "Marriage is honorable, in all, and the bed undefiled"—it is blessed by God. It is also in the bible—who God has joined together, let no man put asunder and that a man must leave his mother and father and cleave or stick to his wife, so that the two flesh are to become one (only in child bearing can the two flesh truly becomes physically one, as a fulfillment and that love and feelings towards the couple, makes one spiritually into one flesh).

First, let us consider the meaning of marriage, which I will give not from a dictionary, but from common-sense concept, as it should really be. Marriage should be sincere, honest and loyal love for each other and not just a public show. On the other hand documentary marriage is not necessary it is beyond state paper works, for it is to be welded and molded as seen above, that the two flesh are to become one and no more as in the single, for a man or a woman to think that their flesh belongs to themselves, but rather, it is to be equally shared to each other. It is for better or for worse, for rich or for poor, in health or in sickness, till death there is to be a separation.

Depending on the love binding or ties, the parties may patiently wait the processing of marriage, while with others who are impatient, will find the girl getting away (eloping) with the boy, with very little encouragement from him.

Marriage could be regarded as the final stage of bringing the two lovers together and has now become open, fully known and accepted. This is, of course simply confirming or sealing all the fore-runner bargains or promise etc. of the first and second stages (love and courtship) here, is the opportunity, where all or as much as possible, the promises made are being fulfilled and life changes adaptable styles are being practiced. The future holds not much for yourself and wife, but it is the preparation and storage ground for your children. It is hopeful, that later in your life history, when you may inherit the sweat of your brow.

An English marriage (or a Christian) is always a legal one. It is also possible, with other religious body. No doubt, all marriages are legal depending on laws and regulations of the land where it is created. Thus, a marriage application format has to be filled out and tendered. Thereafter a permission or marriage license will be issued for the two persons to marry, should there be no impediment to the marriage.

The Bride will choose brides-maids, preferable from among her sisters, those of the bridegroom or her best friends, but they should all be unmarried. The first bridesmaid has to be taken to church by the best man and she will wait in the porch for the arrival of the bride and will follow her closely with the other bridesmaids, following behind in pairs. She stands at the left at the left of the bride, ready to attend and assist her when the occasions arise. This bridesmaid will proceed to the vestry on the left arm of the best man where the signing of the register and marriages certificate will be done In the presence of the witnesses.

Following to the Vestry, in this order are the other bridesmaids, parents and grandparents. Any dear and special friend and in the same order, they will pass down the aisle out of the church, where they will be assisted in to the waiting car by the Best-man. The bride's father will take the bride to church and in his arm (right) graciously walk the bride down the aisle to the waiting bridegroom and of course, place her at his left side.

The ceremony starts and the father or a brother or other elderly male relative, or whoever takes her to the church will do the giving away of the bride. After placing the bride to-be left side of the groom, he will then step back a little, awaiting the Priest to start and when he reaches the point of asking, who will give the bride away? The bride's father will then answer "I will." Thereafter, he could go and have a seat in the front pew on the left side. Also, the mother, who is escorted by the son or a male relative to church, is seated at the left side of the nave or main part of the church in the front pew with her husband.

The groom's parent will occupy the right side and so are his relatives and friends. After the open-church ceremony, the bride's father, the Bride and groom should be the first to arrive at the reception place, so as to receive or greet their guests and friends and other invitees.

Please remember that the bride will fix the date of the wedding because that option is given to her, so as to avoid her wedding falling on, or during her menstrual cycle. The bride is to provide the bridal outfits, accessories etc. except the bouquet and ring. You will fully guided by the priest about the procedure of the marriage rites which include publishing of banns etc., before the wedding day.

Just before the wedding commences on the wedding day, the officiating Priest would make the last or final announcement (publishing of Bans) and would ask, if anyone has any objections for the couple to marry. If no objections are raised, then the priest will call on all present to forever hold their peace. Thereafter, the wedding ceremony will start. The publishing of the banns will be for three consecutive Sundays. The Priest would say "I publish the banns of marriage between John and Susan, if any of you know the cause or just impediment why these two persons should not be joined together in holy matrimony; you are to declare it now. This is the first (second and third times) of asking. At the last publishing of the banns that priest would say, "if any man can show any just causes why they may not lawfully be joined together, let him now speak or else hereafter, forever hold his peace".

Although, age is no barrier to passionate love, after maturity, it is always better and also looks well in society, when choosing a partner. The age should be on the balance scale and as tradition have it from ancient times, one must not be too old or too young less you will be tantalized that you marry your father, your grandfather or your mother or grandmother respectively. The man, as society has it, is to be older than the woman. However, there are cases where the woman happened to be the older and also parties of equal age group. It is suggested, that the man should be between two to ten years older than the woman because beyond that, later in life, the man's health and energy will deteriorate at a faster rate than the woman and this could very well end up in problems and unfaithfulness on the woman's part. There are many other sayings to this age grouping, but they are not useful to be mentioned herein.

The married ring is not necessary a plain ring, as is often thought but rather a plain gold—ring (that is, not mixed gold used to make it).

Practically, every type of married sex problems and every age treated and these could be solved and therefore, thereafter experience the supreme satisfaction of a longer, happier married sex life and thus, abolish the lurking danger of worn sex notions. Perhaps, this book will help you to establish the necessary desired cooperation between husband and wife.

The leaning thought of the wife, should be that she loves to get to bed with her husband and there is no better feelings in the world, as exciting and exquisite as having a satisfying intercourse with a man (husband) who, has full possession of his wife. You will love the feelings of intercourse, those moments of expectations with increased tension, as he approaches with searching stabs of entry into the vagina and finally, the still and motionless moments. All that rises, from the shock of the togetherness of pleasures.

Man's pride, prestige and ability rest in his genital improvements, by which the female will express gratitude in satisfaction. Every woman and every man admires a fine female figure, of which the breasts indeed, greatly assist to display the beauty. Perhaps, previously, such subjects have been avoided purely through shame and to a great extent through ignorance. The shame is rooted even today between husbands and wives. You will be surprised; to learn should you question a husband or wife about each other, how little they know each other sexually. This lack of knowledge and misfortunes are caused and so, we have a broken home.

As you may notice in many religious cultures, at wedding ceremony, you the female were either tied (nuptial knot) at the back of your husband and he led you. This reminds you that this (he) is the leader and head over you. In other cases, you were hooked up abreast at his side and this reminds you of equality and perhaps, you were led to believe that you are equal to him. You must this day see the missing dimension, which is, that you were hooked to his left side and not on his right, while he was to your right. This shows that you have only part equality, while he has in his command, full authority over you. You do not have equal rights over him and that your equality is left (wrong or right) maybe, to be equal and to be an overseer. Danger lies there in ambush for you.

As I conclude here, I wish to leave with you this metaphoric summary illustration which covers this entire book. Please try to understand it carefully for it is useful but how valuable? You are the reader and practitioner alone could confirm this information.

Life is based on these masters. Can you escape them? Just try!

HABIT: Ha-bit

MANAGEMENT: Man-age-ment (old)

ASSUME: ass-u-me (Me is an ass or me and U is an Ass)

Habit; Management; Assume = Time

TIME: ti-me (TIE ME)

So, it is meant that man will get age and HA (cry of surprise) as
an ass, he will have to wear a BIT and that goes for U (you) and
ME.

CHAPTER 10

Menstruation, Menopause, Expectancy and Menstrual Cycle

In this table, I will try to alert the female when to expect menstruation and when it is expected to stop, which is known as "change of life" or menopause or when the flowering period would have come to an end and so it is with child bearing. Notice that some young girls, who matured early, will start to menstruate early.

Year menstruation maybe expected	Year menopause maybe expected
10 years	50-52 years
11	48-50
12	46-48
13	44-46
14	42-44
15	40-42
16	38-40
17	36-38
18	34-36
19	32-34
20	30-32

This table is to serve as a guide and there may be variations. The onset of menopause brings on some discomfort, which may vary, with the female in degree. While some may not suffer from all these fore-runners. Fail not, however to consult your doctor for guidance.

There may be constipation, physical discomfort, and mild mental and nervous changes with some women. While, some women cease menstruation with slight inconveniences. As a rule the woman may miss a few—one, two or more periods, then menstrual period will reappear to almost normal or reduce flow for a period and then disappear and re-appear again and this may go on for within two years when it will cease completely.

The menstrual cycle is the guideline for what is called the safety or danger periods, pertaining to sexual intercourse and conception. I will attempt to provide you with these guidelines. If a woman menstruates on regular bases, every 28 days, it will usually be impossible for her to conceive between the first and tenth day of her menstrual cycle. Checking from the first day the menstrual flow begins, she could conceive between the 11th to the 17th day of the menstrual cycle starts if you do want a baby, and you are to have natural sexual intercourse during this period.

The system is that on the 14th of each menstrual cycle, ripe eggs will be released from the ovaries. So fertilization of the egg or eggs in cases of twins, could take place in the fallopian tube, by a live male sperm on the 14th, 15th or 16th because the male sperm will not survive for more than seventy-two hours. Hence the egg contacts with the sperm after that will be of no value.

I will provide you with a few more normal examples, so that the usual variations that will show up from time to time be taken care of, nor will it meet you in surprise. To avoid unawareness and amazement the forecast pregnancy chart has been provided along with the calculation method which can be used with some degree of accuracy, which is more or less due to variation or failure of the mother-to-be to provide accurate checking information.

Menstruation 1   Ovulation 1   Journey through fallopian tube to

               Starts 14   to womb ends

                             21 28

                          To start again

Remember due to variation of dates and the menstrual cycle maintaining the ratio, these few more e.g. as stated above becomes necessary for your guide.

Suggested menstruation commence	Ovulation date discharge of ripen eggs from ovaries	Time taken for eggs to travel through the fallopian tube and reach the womb 14 days
1st-5th	14th	28
1st-4th	14th	28
1st-5th	12th	26
1st-5th	13	27
1st-5th	15	29
1st-5th	18th	32—next month

It can be seen, that the shortest menstrual period is the 26th and the longest 32nd, which would mean to go over to another month and this would then call for a different calculation and so, too ovulation has the variation of taking place on the 12th as being the shortest and on the 18th, as being the longest. Conception shortest cycle would be three days—seventy-two hours, on either side of the 12th equal 9th to 15th and on the longest cycle; it would be three days on either side of 18th, which would be 15th to 21st.

Roughly, this diagram will help you to understand, what has been explained above.

Menstruation	Abstain—keepaway from coitus, if no pregnacy is to happen	Safe period when no conception will take place
1th-5th	9th-21th	26th-32nd
	On the other hand if a child is needed then have sex during this period	Free to have coitus

How you could estimate expected childbirth. This will depend how accurate the expectant mother could provide the date. However, whatever the circumstances, the method would remain and so in nine months by calendar counting, and ten months, 280 days lunar.

Normal, unvaried and uninterrupted cycle—regular.

(1) Say the last menstruation period is—October 14, 1995

    Calculation Method:
    Period when it becomes known, minus month 3, plus 1 year
    i.e: 10-3+1 =7/24/96
This is the short period explained.

(2) The long period cycle, which goes into another month, although slightly different the system will take the same pattern.

    Late menstrual period:
    May 25, 1995

Add 10 days and 1 month:

10+1 - (25+10=35)

Hence revert to the above or first method by no further adding 10 days which was already done but will now deal with the month and the year so, take away 3 months and add 1 year.

BRIEFING ON CONCEPTION

MAN			**Woman**		
Produces both Body cells	Make up of body cells		Produce single female cells		
X	Y		X	X	CHROMOSOME
FEMALE	MALE	CHROMOSOME	FEMALE	FEMALE	
IN MAM SPERM			IN WOMAM OVA		
FEMALE	MALE		FEMALE	FEMALE	
X	Y		X	X	
MALE CHILD			FEMALE CHILD		

Month	31	30	29	28	27	26	25	24	23	22	21	20	19	18	17	16	15	14	13	12	11	10	9	8	7	6	5	4	3	2	1
January	31	30	29	28	27	26	25	24	23	22	21	20	19	18	17	16	15	14	13	12	11	10	9	8	7	6	5	4	3	2	1
Ocotober	7	6	■	■	■	2	1	31	30	29	28	27	26	25	24	23	22	21	20	19	18	17	16	15	14	13	12	11	10	9	8
February	■	■	29	28	27	26	25	24	23	22	21	20	19	18	17	16	15	14	13	12	11	10	9	8	7	6	5	4	3	2	1
November	■	■	5	4	3	2	1	31	30	29	28	27	26	25	24	23	22	21	20	19	18	17	16	15	14	13	12	11	10	9	8
March	31	30	29	28	27	26	25	24	23	22	21	20	19	18	17	16	15	14	13	12	11	10	9	8	7	6	5	4	3	2	1
December	5	4	3	2	1	31	30	29	28	27	26	25	24	23	22	21	20	19	18	17	16	15	14	13	12	11	10	9	8	7	6
April	■	30	29	28	27	26	25	24	23	22	21	20	19	18	17	16	15	14	13	12	11	10	9	8	7	6	5	4	3	2	1
January	■	4	3	2	1	31	30	29	28	27	26	25	24	23	22	21	20	19	18	17	16	15	14	13	12	11	10	9	8	7	6
May	31	30	29	28	27	26	25	24	23	22	21	20	19	18	17	16	15	14	13	12	11	10	9	8	7	6	5	4	3	2	1
February	6	5	4	3	2	1	31	30	29	28	27	26	25	24	23	22	21	20	19	18	17	16	15	14	13	12	11	10	9	8	7
June	■	30	29	28	27	26	25	24	23	22	21	20	19	18	17	16	15	14	13	12	11	10	9	8	7	6	5	4	3	2	1
March	■	4	3	2	1	31	30	29	28	27	26	25	24	23	22	21	20	19	18	17	16	15	14	13	12	11	10	9	8	7	6
July	31	30	29	28	27	26	25	24	23	22	21	20	19	18	17	16	15	14	13	12	11	10	9	8	7	6	5	4	3	2	1
April	6	5	4	3	2	1	31	30	29	28	27	26	25	24	23	22	21	20	19	18	17	16	15	14	13	12	11	10	9	8	7
August	31	30	29	28	27	26	25	24	23	22	21	20	19	18	17	16	15	14	13	12	11	10	9	8	7	6	5	4	3	2	1
May	6	5	4	3	2	1	31	30	29	28	27	26	25	24	23	22	21	20	19	18	17	16	15	14	13	12	11	10	9	8	7
September	■	30	29	28	27	26	25	24	23	22	21	20	19	18	17	16	15	14	13	12	11	10	9	8	7	6	5	4	3	2	1

June	8	9	10	11	12	13	14	15	16	17	18	19	20	21	22	23	24	25	26	27	28	29	30	1	2	3	4	5	6	7	
October	1	2	3	4	5	6	7	8	9	10	11	12	13	14	15	16	17	18	19	20	21	22	23	24	25	26	27	28	29	30	31
JUly	8	9	10	11	12	13	14	15	16	17	18	19	20	21	22	23	24	25	26	27	28	29	30	31	1	2	3	4	5	6	7
November	1	2	3	4	5	6	7	8	9	10	11	12	13	14	15	16	17	18	19	20	21	22	23	24	25	26	27	28	29	30	
Augnust	8	9	10	11	12	13	14	15	16	17	18	19	20	21	22	23	24	25	26	27	28	29	30	31	1	2	3	4	5	6	
December	1	2	3	4	5	6	7	8	9	10	11	12	13	14	15	16	17	18	19	20	21	22	23	24	25	26	27	28	29	30	31
September	7	8	9	10	11	12	13	14	15	16	17	18	19	20	21	22	23	24	25	26	27	28	29	30	1	2	3	4	5	6	7

Above is a forecast pregnancy chart showing dates of expected Birth of Child in relation to time of conception. The top line date, shown the first day of the last menstruation before pregnancy. The date underneath is the assumed date when the baby should born. The baby may born within two weeks before or after, it should not exceed 280 days date of conception, if it is known by the mother to be.

Menopause Or Change Of Life

Both men and women are greeted with this un-escapable period in life, and its effect could be the deciding factor for the future from menopause to death, as to whether you will continue to enjoy a normal intimate relationship. Thus, the effect and causes for concern, are more conspicuous (attracting attention) among women. I would place more emphasis on the female side in this matter and although I cannot deal with it fully, enough is disclosed to guide and prepare you for this, your lap in the matrimonial race.

You cannot afford to fall out or fail to perform and lose your stripes of credit-worthiness at this stage. Where are you going to look for it and if found, to restore it? This book will attempt to help you to do so.

Menopause or change of life ceases and mark the end of the flowering and child bearing period, although there are a few, as I understand exceptionally rare conception cases on record. After this period, and further within your menstruation period, if the menstruation is absent, you must be reminded that you could still conceive, just as well, you could still be seeing your menstruation and is left with a child. These are however, rare cases and that there are other factors on which could rely on to be in the known on the above.

Menopause may happen more commonly between that ages of thirty or forty years and rarely in the fifties, although, it could be earlier or later, depend on the individual's health. It is not an intruder and does not step in on you suddenly, but may show signs of this transition period, which may last or vary between two to three years. The symptoms are:

- Hot flashes, which may last up to thirty minutes.
- Feelings of fatigue.
- Mild joint pain.
- Feelings of depression.
- Irritability.
- Increase flow of menstruation.
- Generally, it will become less and less until it stops altogether.

- At times, a cold or chilly sensation will be felt.
- Loss or gain in weight.
- Appetite may increase or decrease.
- Nausea, vomiting, fainting and dizziness.
- Palpitation of the heart.
- Backache and headache.
- Diarrhea or constipation.
- Almost, any of the health troubles that the individual woman had earlier in life, and had ceased, may begin again with some or all of the above symptoms with the onset of these you should promptly consult with your doctor, who will up-date you and be willing to help you.

The first change for a woman (girl) is puberty, when the menstruation begins and finally, ends at menopause. It is natural and inescapable, so it is nothing to fear, but rather it is better to know what to expect and when to start get ready including what should be done to help and that your marital life-style and relationship are not jeopardized. In most cases the husband being a few years older, as a result, the menopause period for both husband and wife, may occur within the same period or not far apart. Both parties may develop a few different attitudes towards each other, which may result in danger, if not properly handled.

At this crucial point, the walls of the vagina become thinner, drier and less elasticity so sexual intercourse could be uncomfortable and so the wife loss interest and even the husband may not have an enjoyable satisfaction. However it could be readily enjoyed, by applying any suitable and agreeable lubricant such as honey, oil or cream.

The erotic centers of both men and women are the big-toes, feet, heels, knees, pelvis, navel, chest, breast, abdomen, back, arm-pits, throat, cheeks, lips, tongue, eyes, forehead, head, legs and the sex organs of the female herself. For men, the right side of the body and for women the left side of the body is to be fondled and careful manipulations and tender touching of these sensitive and sex conscious centers will arouse love. Lubricate the vagina and place one in heat, thus causing her to seek fulfillment in actual intercourse.

During the day the above manipulations are to done from head to toe, while at night from toe to head. Sexual intercourse could cover approximately sixty-four or more fascinating artful embraces and positions, all of which you will discover for yourself.

I need not treat them here. You must however, gracefully indulge in the aforesaid foreplay and love making. Your front line defender of a happy sex relation coupled with the above in this your golden and diamond years are—outdoor exercise, light work, plenty of sleep, cold water bath and ice-water during hot flashes, wholesome and balance diet, multivitamins and female hygiene regularly, all of which will encourage the upper level of estrogen, which is in short supply at menopause. It is also suggested, that you must not wait until the appointed time but to embark on these disclosed information well in advance of the expected menopause period particularly, that you now have an idea of it.

During And After the Menopause Period

There is several feeling of discomfort, pains and headache etc. Are due, because the usual wastage and its courses of emptying has to be diverted and hared up plus taken over and cared for by the other purifying organs and when this is regularized, all things being equal, your health will return to normal. Possibly you have to male most of it while there is life.

It is not the end as many females may think. But rather, it is the beginning of a more free marital life and life style for there is no more messy menstruation, coupled with the child bearing burden and caring inclusive of precautions and the many restrictions which bar your many actions and movements. This, your ending through the home-stretch lap, could be just as sweet, happy and enjoyable as your beginning. Should you follow the rightful maneuvers, all of which would be found in this book.

Here are some natural help found in sex stimulant food—egg white provide protein, oysters, clam skin fish and other sea foods, these provide iodine, red peppers, garlic, cheese and chili powder, hot spices cause urethral irritation and bring about more indulging. Beans, milk liver etc. broccoli, whole wheat bread, nuts, pumpkinseeds, vitamin B complex group and vitamin E.

DIET: 3 eggs for breakfast, steak for lunch and fish for supper.

How To Make up a Diet

Liver once per week, fish or seafood twice a week, eggs once a day, six slices of whole wheat daily, citrus fruit daily, green and yellow vegetables and one pint of milk daily.

CHAPTER 11

Naming of the Child

First, you write down the following information, dealing with the birth of the child, say day—Wednesday, date—20th, November 1963. Next step form the given table, check for the number and alphabet and you must write them down as per the given example, by this method you could interpret anything, words into letters and letters into numbers, phases, sentences, dreams, etc. Those values were being used in the ancient times and even to this day by people all over the world, who appreciate it. E.g. Kabalists, Rascerucians, Indians, Africans, etc.

This is the English alphabetical system. It has some variations from the Hebrew, are not Hebrews, however, notwithstanding this, I had also included the Hebrew system.

ENGLISH TABLE NO. 1			
1	A	J	S
2	B	K	T
3	C	L	U
4	D	M	V
5	E	N	W
6	F	O	X

HEBREW TABLE NO. 2				
1	A	I	J	Q	Y
2	B	C	K	R	
3	G	L	P	S	
4	D	M		T	
5	E	N			
6	U	V	W	X	

7	G	P	Y		7	O	Z
8	H	Q	Z		8	F	H
9	I	R					

WORKING EXAMPLES:

DAY: = Wednesday
            5+5+4+5+5+1+4+1+7
            = 37 = 3+7
            =10 =1+0=1

DATE: 20   =2+0 =2
MONTH   = NOVEMBER
            5+6+4+5+4+2+5+9
            = 40 = 4+0= 4
YEAR   = 1963 = 1+9+6+3 =19
            = 1+9 = 10 = 1+0 = 1
TOTAL   = 1+2+4+1 = 8

By working method, 8 is the final number, again look at 8 in the table, you will find H, Q, Z. The name must now begin with the letters H or Q or Z and when you check out the given or chosen name you are to get the number 8, again e.g. say, your intended or chosen name for the child is Helen, the number will be

H E L E N: 8+5+3+5+5 = 26 = 2+6 = 8

Now this is her lucky name and number. I do hope you will not find it difficult when working out your name from the table.

CHAPTER 12

Sterile Or Barrenness

Barrenness among men and women are some few in percentage to the human race and even some that may be regarded as sterile persons, could be medically treated successfully with their deficiencies—maybe, hormone. It is advisable for both persons to consult a doctor, who, will examine and no doubt know what will be required whether treatment or advise.

There are some cases, where a cleaning of the womb may serve the purpose and this could only be determined and no doubt solved through a doctor. It is advisable to do so as early as possible. However, there are some people who get children later in life. In some known cases, experienced old people treated at home and some of these unfortunate ones happened to response favorable. Some experienced that change of partner's help that is the husband took another wife and the wife likewise took another husband and they got children, with their new partners.

I cannot at this point decide for you, this will surely have to be between yourself and partner. It is on these occasions, that true love is put to the test and agreement suitable to both sides, is arrived at. Here is a safe and proven old people method, that I learnt about and unfortunately, I never had the opportunity to try it out. It is said that, if a woman is not getting children, she should chew approximately five to seven sunflower seeds first thing in the mornings for about a month or to such extended period, until she is successful. At the same time, the husband must experiment while having sexual relations with his wife, during the period conception is possible and is elsewhere described In this book.

Please check the safety period charts and to make sure you have sexual fulfillment during the right period which described as the danger period for conception that will be three days before and three days after ovulation. Having determined the date menstruation, it will be fourteen days thereafter, in a normal and regular twenty-eight days menstrual cycle.

CHAPTER 13

Adolescent and Parents

This chapter on youth is important for both parents and children, for it is that period of molded partnership and relationship between parents and children.

The meaning of adolescent is basically young boys and girls from puberty to adulthood, perhaps in their teens. Growing up, developing for childhood to maturity. The quality of being youthful juvenile.

In the present day generation, great emphasis and rightly so, is placed on youth and among the importance about the youth of today is the man and woman of tomorrow. They will then be the deciders of the future and this statement, being true, must be taken into account of how interested are these youths to be responsible persons in the nation building which could be a story with a different color. However, this cannot be avoided, whether the elders like it or not. Parents must be prepared for a peaceful transition though teaching to their children.

This growth and changes in stature etc., thus developing the youths is assessed to be from thirteen years average for girls and average fifteen years for boys with perfectly normal health who, matures earlier or later from this given average age. It is difficult for them to make sensible adjustments between this age group and the growth rate is rapid, but is drastically slows down after the average age of twenty.

Good health would largely depend on plenty of quality food and sleep plus a good deal of physical exercise, taking care not to be excessive in anything. There will be changes in boy shape and voices, also hair growth and increase of breast. A rounded hips and waistline for girls, while boys will slightly reduce at the waist and hip, but put on a broader shoulder.

After the adolescent period, the once child will have to be prepared and make adjustments, to sever parental attachments and thus learn to adopt oneself to accommodate the many emotional problems as an independent adult.

At this period, one looks to fashion oneself competing with their own group, as a result, reckless and dangerous things are being done. This is more or less due, because of their young friends and advice are far better and important to the adolescent than that given by their parents or guardians. The youth are extremely sensitive to criticism and they resent any outsider suggestions and crown himself that his or her age group's opinions are better than those from the parents further, they may behave and even show dislike for parents. It is at this stage an intelligent handling from tactful and sympathetic parents are necessary so as to avoid a chain of crisis.

Here is a useful story: the Chinese, it was said, built a massive defense wall to protect them against the invasion of the enemy's from the north. It could have generally served its purpose. The failure, however, was due because the enemies breached it not by force or mechanical but by merely bribing the gatekeeper, who let them in.

The creator has built his defense wall strong, but he has made us the gatekeeper. It is our mind that is tempted. The will is the target and the real is us. It is therefore seen that the mind is the gatekeeper, which takes or rejects the bribe. How can you, the parent bribe the mind of the youth? You know best, try embarking on it. Perhaps persuasion is better than persecution.

Careful handling from parents, may cause them (parents) to go out of the way temporarily and not a bit wrong from the normal way, in trying to overlook their (youth's) short-comings and may even shower a bit of praise at their accomplishments, if this area will be a solution. The parents will not ask too much in return from adolescent.

People, at all ages have thoughts, feelings and desires and if these were rightly cultivated, then the right behavior would be induced. One will have to become adaptable and fits smoothly and effectively into given situation he finds himself or herself. Youth, failing to pull them together, could and very often result in juvenile delinquency, where or when rule and order are not obeyed and have no meaning even punishment is not a detergent. Parents, it is said, when the child is small, you fill its belly and all is ok, but when he or she gets walking your trouble begins.

Despite the advance education fortunately, at the reach of today's generation, the teenager's dilemma, is on the increase because they feel they are more educated than the parents hence, parental advises, guidelines and teachings are inferior and they ignore and throw their parents offerings in the wayside dumps as rubbish.

It is a generation of rapid changes, on the move to keep a pace with panic and passion of the society. The voice resentments protest and rebellions in nature, riot is their possession and they are easily led astray at this stage, although, truly the homes of tomorrow are in their hands. Of course, they keep asking themselves, "can the thunderstorms in the youth's heart ceased, before it is too late? Surprisingly, they gain sympathy from other elderly citizen and this boosts their conduct.

Dear parents, boys and girls, love is given equally to all to circulates not to waste but to replace hate. It is the only ingredient that mixes and meshes any-how and fits anywhere, anytime and does destroys hate completely. You cannot buy, beg, steal or borrow it because you have it always with you. Therefore, do not allow hate to overtake love. It is themost precious nectar given to us freely. To suppress it, would destroy the homes. So as to sever relationships between parents, children, husbands, wives, brothers, sisters, other relatives and people as a whole, even life itself. It has neither substitute nor limitation in our lives.

Parents or guardians, please accept that at this crucial point of the young's life, only love could manage in rough and troubled times. In molding the adolescent, do not be too hasty but firm and cautious. Do not hurl abuse, insults, silly remarks and criticisms, all of which are unnecessary and most parents are guilty of this approach, when dealing with the child. This is a stage when both your love and patience not your emotional upsetting is on trial and is put to the test. The knowledge, you personally gain from your youthful days and now, your adulthood and as parents, shall be useful. You are at this point and time given the opportunity to put it into practice and then look on to see how successful you are and what fruits your ideas and system bears.

The adolescent stage is when the young grown-up wants to go independent and charter his or her own course. Their maps and compasses could be the ideas, customs and practices of their parents or that of which they selected from the open world, environment and neighborhood. Parents will have to be tactful as to send the youth rightly as an independent one in the open world. This is the time when they will have to keep faith because grief will fill their hearts to sever the unbiblical cord of togetherness. Hence, because you have a fairly good knowledge of what the young man or woman will have to face out there, when they are not well groomed, properly prepared and soundly grounded with the sparks of fire, that is flying as fireworks out there.

Parents, you are to remember that the young grown-ups will have to be on their own, and independent one day. You may not always be around in their joys or difficulties and although, you are filled with grief, you have a great responsibility to set that aside and bless the children and send them with the right foot forward.

As much advice as possible are to be given to them, so that when they set sail, there will be no surprises to cross their path and that with diligent searching, they could press the button of solution. They will always remember that the parents had given at least the guidelines as to the mountains, valleys and level planes through life's journey. Children are a handed down treasures from generation to generation, you, as parents can and must do your best for the young at this extremely trying period. It is known that it would not be an easy task because the young grown-ups will show a lot of resistance to your good advice and intentions, but frustration must not be allowed to enter and deal a heavy blow, although it will be constantly rapping at the door.

Please be careful and be cautious dear parents, because you also can be confused from the type of reception and response the child will give and besides their management, you do have the routine of your own management affairs and over-all responsibilities. It is under stood that you have to take on the extra two directions that now present themselves at this point in your life.

- A grieved hearts because the child wants to be free independent and takes his or her own decisions.
- The onset of teaching the youth of what the open world has to share to him or her, particularly, at the time, when the child will love to take his or her own way and would care less of what you do advise. This is a delicate situation indeed, and must be treated with the care and attention it deserves.

Believe it or not, we were all rebuttal to our parents at this youthful stage. Now as we are realizing, our then mistakes later in life, the greater our desire from our own experiences would want to prevent our children from making the same regrettable errors. The greater our mistakes, the wider our experiences and because of the parental love they do not want their children to fall into those pits. However, no matter what care you take, they are going to make the very mistakes to a greater or lesser extent and so, will be impact, depending on how much they accede and display the given guidelines.

Very often, your children may give back answers, grumbles and rudeness. You may hear remarks from them such as "you had your days and time, you did the same things and even worst, it's our time, why not give us a chance, why not watch-man us?" Among the few of what will hurl to you. Regardless, of what, you as parents have to endure, remain sincere, loyal and faithful to your off-springs, in due course, they will select what they want from what you disclosed to them.

Most young men and women, plunge into the swift moving waters of tomorrow, and find themselves at this exciting adventure and moments into a straight road which lead into a living hell. Perhaps, in less than a year for example, marriage, candle light and romance soon burns out. What is it that shatters the in-expressible joy of the wedding day or even at the arrival of the newborn baby of your desire. These joys and anxieties do not have to come apart in midstream.

Success of marriage, although not easy, is possible. It is a do it yourself project. The adolescent are to remember and take precaution because this spontaneous attraction to the young opposite sex, no doubt, will be the first magnetic pull and at this period they mostly go astray and are easily enticed into what appears to them, the best the world have to offer. I wonder if this poem could help and be a guiding beacon.

Love is not passion or hate;
Love is not pride;
Love is not a journey side by side;
Arms in arms, not of the breeze nor of the gale;
Love is the steady set of the soul;
Deeper than ecstasy, sweeter than light;
Born in sunshine, born in night;
Flaming is victory, strongest in loss;
Love is sacrament, made for a cross.

Very often, we have to be careful thoughts for strangers and sweet smiles for the visiting guests, but often for our own, the bitter tone. Do not allow your holy wedlock to be transformed into unholy deadlock. Are these good and sound advises? Then, follow them and if you do, they are invaluable, then ignore them. Do follow the better of the two streams.

Well, I tell you my young friends, there is a recipe at the time of need and it is no doubt found in this book. Say something nice to those you happen to contact or have dealings with. Why not drink from the golden chalice of friendship and love; rather from the brazen cup of duty. The challenges ahead, are not only finding in the right person. Try to make people happy rather than good. We can succeed if only the hard work and dedication, we put into any job slaving for others. We should really put into our homes.

What is tact? You may ask. Simply, it is saying and doing in the right way the right things, at the right time and in the right place to the right person with the right tone of voice in the right mood in the right atmosphere with the right motive in the right mind. Should there be a savage contest with each trying to wound more deeply, than the other, then there bound to be a crisis and you will be picked up at the other end of the flowing stream badly wounded in sorrow. Too late shall be the cry because no quarrel is good, let it be done instead, by meaningful discussions, with the hope for an amicable solution.

The man can avoid the matrimonial-ship from tossing. If, as a father all he can do for the children is to love their mother and there will be domestic tranquility and contentment among all. Do not cause the heart to drain wastefully its good desires. Your corner stone is communication and this is an excellent vehicle. So, as to heal the rift and bridge the gulf. The circuit jammers between parents or guardians and the youths are the perfectionist system within us all. This means that if parents are wrong, they are still right and the child is always wrong and the child on the other hand feels that they are always right and the parent is wrong. Of course, to both parents and the young, this perfectionist system is going to mess everything. Therefore, neither party is to adopt it. It would foster a bitter relationship that could explode or get broken at any time when you least expect it.

Parents, children relationship, must be quickly and solidly re-anchored and should leave no deep scars. We must say, "I am wrong" when it is so or maybe, if it is the only way that an agreement could be reached and you are to say "I love you" when it warrants these words of healing. Do not hesitate and ponder too long, it could harbor danger especially, to an upset and blind emotional mind.

Grown up, children, please remember that respect of parents is a true sign of refinement and surely no matter how old, big or educated you are, you are still your parent's child. Having read what is suggested herein and that you do make use of them. I am confident that the teenager will approach and get over this introductory period more smoothly. At the same time, the parents or guardians of the teenager would deal with the situations more skillfully with less fearful incidents and both sides will be more confident of success in their respective role.

Through this probationary period and your apprenticeship, you must not be frightening monster to either parties but it will be filled with adventures and excitements. A bad introduction could very well be damaging, leaving a deep scar for life, which will cause the teenager and parents many sad regrets. Both sides are to be careful and cultivate determination to make things work together for their common goal and good purpose. Although, these achievements are rare, it is possible to gain through the outlined step by step facts brought out herein to both the parents and the teenager.

This is the trial and mistake period. You could learn from your mistakes as well as from other people's mistakes. It could be a valuable stepping stone and maybe, when confronted with the adverse happenings you can either make or break it because, all matters are in your hands and resting squarely on your shoulders.

Advice could only be shared to you and with you but, the application and working strain continues to rest with you, personally and your forth coming success would largely depend on what you put into practice in this most interesting project. How strong will you both build your super-structure and on what foundation including the type of materials to be used in this revolving world? So, as to avoid being thrown over the precipice for life would base on the sound plans you have formulated and your genuine, not necessary rigid implementation of it for the sustainable growth and expansion in several fields.

Teenager, while you can and should ask questions, you are to avoid being argumentative, less your good intentions could be foiled and shattered to pieces and then you would have been sailing in a sinking ship. Should you capsize this ship and you are not a good swimmer, then you could very well be drowned, if no one goes to you rescue. Remember this is what your parent or guardian is doing or should do for you. On the other hand, should you navigate well although, you may have a leaking vessel, your riding voyage will be sweet and enjoyable and your destination will be safe to shore. There will be no more room for mushrooming disappointment or regrets.

Youngsters, play it cool. What has passed is gone is history, but the future is coming for it is straight ahead of you. So build your barns large enough as though you are preparing for a life time famine and if it does not appear, then, good luck and this is exactly what I wish both parents and teenagers as I bring this chapter to a close.

CHAPTER 14

Masturbation

It all started when the young boys or even, grown up men have an erection and they placed their hands on their penis, thereby fondling or play with it. As they continuing doing this, they gradually get a moment of feeling good, which urges them to continue the movements at their own adjustable pace which set them to the emotion and thus, climax and ejaculate. With this emotion of feeling good, they are inclined to continue with such a pleasure.

The sexual organs, react automatically and have being aroused, one gets into motion, with the sexual juices flowing. The wonderful feelings increases and, the female, like the male place her fingers on the clitoris which responds to her movements, whereby she gets an enjoyable and satisfactory orgasm. These enjoyments are the encourager to masturbation then, and in the future.

Ignorance, physiological guilt and shame, coupled with mis-information are some of the sexual problems, which restrict many young girls and maybe, even the older women, from having adequate sexual relationships. To a great extent, mothers are responsible for most of these unwarranted situations, just because they fail, either through their ignorance or their high class level of living, to rightly advice or guide and share their gained experiences to their grown up daughters. As a result, a very poor introduction is given to an enjoyable and the most enjoyable sex life.

Girls, of this kind are very doubtful of their purpose in sex life and to satisfy their curiosity, they either become rejected and unresponsive, or go at it, thus taking a long time by their trials and errors, with embarrassments, as to what a man may think of them. Whether, they are the right type or not, and if they meet all the requirements that a man may need or look for. Some, make success while, others have gone astray in their determination to cover this field.

A woman wants to be credited by her husband, that she had displayed the best all-round qualities above all other women, to her husband's satisfaction. But she is ashamed to fully discuss her sexual actions or performances, with her husband or to what extent she had pleased him throughout the activities, before leading up to and during and after intercourse. The problem is after a fulfillment, each partner quickly turns it their normal activities. If it is during the day, or if it is during the night, they turn their backs to each other, or even remove from that bed to another. But no discussion whatsoever goes on over what they have done. Maybe, to them it is a sin or some sort of evil to do. The wife will never ask her husband if she had satisfied him or did she live up to his expectations, or how she was enjoyed sexually or that she could be seen as the pride of his heart etc. The husband, will neither think or express to her a few words of credit, but rather, they both will obey the traffic sign" no noise", "silent zone"

I am afraid that all of these expose the mother, where their daughters, because of lack of training and information, looks to sexual intercourse as a crime and as a result, at times these hungry girls, seek redress through their own age group friends. Who are not knowledgeable developed in this important area.

Many mother, discriminate against their childhood daughters which is a sad consequences, for they are only told, the dark side of life, pattern and behavior such as not to touch or play with vagina. "It is ugly, dirty and smells bad. The only thing to be done is to just wash it and not even look at it." However, on the contrary, it is advisable that the grown—ups, inclusive of the elderly, should look at themselves, using a mirror regularly, especially when there is something wrong and before going to the doctor.

There is no cause to be ashamed or scorn yourself. A check shows that a large percentage of women are guilty of the above, and never become familiar with their own faces, images or shapes. Some may only try to look at their faces during make-up and dressing time and the part that is most important, is neglected. It must be remembered that your part is the beginning of the human race, which populates the world and at the same time provides comforting satisfaction for both, women and men. You will notice that I dealt with that part at the time of copulation by both parties elsewhere.

It may be hard to believe, but my opinion is that approximately 98 % of men and women had masturbated sometime, somewhere through life's journey. It is also true that some have done it more frequently that others, even in marriage lie, it happens to be indulged in. There are some that for the first time may have done masturbation, innocently or accidentally.

Wet dreams happen to every man and woman, who is sexually alive sometimes through life, early or late. It is not a sick and is an automatic release, discharge or ejaculation which takes place while you are asleep and dream of having sexual intercourse with someone. On awakening, you find yourself wet.

It will however, be on a reduction scale after marriage or after one has a regular sexual partner.

CHAPTER 15

Accessories for Male and Femal Sex Life

This chapter is to provide you with brief information on a few products that can help you to have a healthy sex life. Some of the accessories could be tremendous value to the whole family. In addition it can also help some men and women, who may be experiencing difficulties due to real or imagined sexual inadequacies which, of course would cause a break down in sexual relationships between men and women and this will seriously disrupt family life.

Surely, these mentioned accessories do not pretend to diagnose a genuine fault or illnesses, nor will they treat illnesses. Promptly consult your doctor immediately, if there is a problem beyond your control. However, the intelligent uses of these products can help you and your family to achieve peak health, vitality and excellent performances.

In recent years, there is an alarming increase in men all ages, which admit with depression that they are particularly impotent. That is, they are unable to obtain or maintain a full penis erection, because they soften and fall. If there is a penetration, ejaculation is very fast and the woman is left unsatisfied, thus defeating the purpose of marriage and the sex act.

If sociologist, should carry out a research today, they would find an alarming frequency increase of a new pattern in behavior, toward as marriage and divorce, men and women are openly disregarding traditional motivation or marrying one another and also this pattern place rape on the increase.

Consider carefully and ask the following questions—is it love? No! Is it companionship or mutual career interest? Hardly! Is it because of childhood or school sweetheart, or money? None of these truly apply, although they all play an important role to those who are blind to the true facts at the beginning of love. What then, is it? Sex? Yes! The whole marriage is based on sex.

Of course, the purpose is nothing new. It is just being truthful to each other and although as time goes by with the development of mutual common interest; sex remains the foremost topic and cause. You are lucky to read this book, whereby you become knowledgeable of the dormant facts which are somewhat hidden to others.

Although, their indulgences are there and they are not conscious of their existences. At first it is an intention within the mind to get at the beautiful individual for sexual satisfaction, which arouses love. To get at her you decide to marry and so it is being fulfilled in marriage.

In the past, when there was impotence, this sexual pleasure could not have been met. It was indeed frightening and in desperation, one seeks quack methods, which proved scientifically ineffective, but now a day, modern medicines had tremendously improved the situations. Further, doctors have invented accessories which could help both sexes. Artificial vagina and penis are successfully used, but surely these cannot replace the human natural parts but you must understand that under the unfortunate circumstance, there is nothing you could do about it. Hesitantly, you will have to turn to the artificial method.

There is an energizing ring for men. When worn, it produces a minute electrical current to the sex organ and improves the vigor and stamina of men of all ages because it has revitalizing properties, which renew virility and potency. There is artificial penis, of different sizes but shape exactly as the naked penis. To wear is also the penis support, when in use the padded sheaths could be used. It is made of pliable latex and the penis is to be inserted in it then in the vagina.

There is further a unique vibrator for men and a stimulator developer for men also. For women, are vibrators of different kinds, pelvic ball energizer, stimulant vibrators, artificial hallowed penis and the massage vibrators? May I repeat, no matter how satisfying are these, or their experimental local artificial human sexual parts there is nothing as satisfying as the natural parts and sexual practices.

Now let me look at another sexual pleasure of much concern and that prolongs intercourse by men. Manufacturers had bought many helpful materials which when used by men delay their ejaculation. Some of these drugs are on the market in creams, foams and liquids. They also appear under several brand names. Should these be used or not is the important question.

Here is the solution. I would suggest yes under the following conditions:—

- Because of the delayed action your partner must approve.
- If you are a habitual partner who ejaculates too quickly, and leave your partner incomplete and dis-satisfied.

- Delay ejaculation is necessary at the same time; this must not be overdone.

Why delayed actions must not be practice?

(a) It is dangerous to the woman whose parts become tender and festers. Thus, leaving the partner in pain, in some cases for days. What should be a pleasure is now fear.
(b) Under these conditions she will be afraid to have sex, since it will no longer be enjoyable.
(c) She will get tired and unable to entertain through that lengthy time.
(d) The delayed action will go too long, which will cause her to have many orgasms (break too much) which will cause exhaust her too much and the purpose of an enjoyable sexual intercourse is truly defeated.
(e) It is dangerous also to the man for he will strain his sex organs and muscles.
(f) He will have a feeling to ejaculate (discharge) but nothing will flow and this will happen over and over again before he will ejaculate and due to the strain, blood will flow.

(g) Because of the length of time, the man will also get tired and the result will be loss of the sexual pleasure.

(h) Most men, who use retard drugs for delayed action for either fun or joke, or to spite the women particularly if she has a lot to talk, boasting and laughing at him.

(i) Constant using of drugs to retard ejaculation will later in life shorten your sexual life span.

(j) It is subject to make men impotent early in life. And it may result in no erection even, at an early age, unless the retarding drugs are being used. Most of these preparations do have priorities which a temporary forceful erection and these un-natural means fail later on, what appear to be sweet at first, will be sours and costly later in life.

Should there be a partial impotency then, consult your doctor immediately who will administer the right drugs to assist you. If this happens you have every right to be concerned and you must take every step to have such a situation corrected and possibly early. There will be some time though life, when the sex drive for both men and women will be reduced.

May I insist, that only natural sex acts should be practiced, that is sexual intercourse is to be an intimate genital contact between the man and the woman and there must be a mutual consent between the matured man and woman. Failing this, it could be regarded as rape. All other systems from natural parts provided for such an act is to be regarded as un-natural. There must be no vulgar and obscene acts or indulgences, because the sexual intercourse is an act of blessing and must be treated or done with the privacy, and therefore need to be done in private. It is not a stage display, and therefore, needs no publicity and advertisement. Let it remain pure and decent.

At maturity, the young man and woman no longer remain innocent to worldly affairs between man and woman, although they may not have actually participated in sexual acts. However, they become knowledgeable and are regarded as the saying goes "big people'. Age is therefore no barrier any longer, so, from thereon only respect and manners for the different age group can strongly hold a disciplined fort in the human race of lovemaking and satisfaction in choosing a partner for relationship within the average age group. Young girls may say it; it is better to be an old man's darling than to be a young man's slave. This may be due to the fact that an old man is a more experienced love-maker and treats the mating partner much better than the young man.

Over indulgences in the sex act could be dangerous to your health and this health hazard would no doubt, retaliate in an early depletion of sexual vitality and energy and so a lost in the sex drive. Although the desire will be still there, performance and satisfaction can no longer be fulfilled. In short, do not try to "done the world for the world will done you".

The sad note of departure has popped up its ugly head. It is time to go into retirement. Once a man twice a child. We have to part from this world for the resting-place, which is patiently waiting and to bear our gray head and our weary bones, which by now are ready to leave everything to this sweet enjoyable and happy world. We shall return with empty hands into rest of our souls, never to return here to play a second win-win game.

Although, oral sexual intercourse was indulged in from the very early years of man's existence, I guess somewhat in secret because one maybe, ashamed to disclose it. However, it is very common and is indulged in perhaps, as frequent as vaginal intercourse.

CHAPTER 16

DO'S and DON'TS

S exual intercourse could be had anytime during the day or night, as you may desire. However, it is advisable for the sake of your health to take certain precautions e.g.:

(a) Do not go after her when the place is heated.

(b) Do not force the sex act because it causes strain on the muscles and tension on the nerves and so there will be no true enjoyment.

(c) Do not have sex, when the stomach is full, just after a meal nor should it be done when you are hungry.

(d) It is not wholesome to have sex early hours of the night, because having worked through the day, you may feel tired. It is best to sleep or have a rest before. The best time could be in the later part of the night to early in the morning. The problem here is that one party may feel too sleepy and not have an inclination and it may result in a force act, just to please the aggressive party. I am aware that happy unions in sexual relationships, cause a deep and refreshing sleep to most people and for that reason, the party may immediately as they retire to bed have intercourse and thereafter, dose away quickly. It is wise to choose the best comfortable, suitable and relaxed position at the time of intercourse and it is not wholesome for the female to be on top and you at the bottom. When you do ejaculate, as regulars practice, it causes great strain on the sex organs, which will result in problems immediately or sometimes later on in life. If this is done far apart, just for the fun, it may not cause problems but don't make it a practice.

(e) Do not go to her without first foreplay, for lack of lubrication will result in a strain or fester on the female part and it will never be an enjoyable and satisfying act.

(f) Do not bathe our parts immediately after intercourse because it gives a sudden chill to the heated parts and it will cause a cold, later in life.

(g) Do not have intercourse when the female natural cleansing period is on. This menstruation period is necessary and the female part is then tender so, you may sore her with most people pain is being felt. The degree varies with some people. Sexual intercourse could be done is not encourages to do so. It happens through life that some people knowingly did it at times with others it was accidentally done.

(h) Do not be drunk in the sex act and behave as an animal, remember the female is a human being and has tender feelings. The act is not something evil. Nothing evil must be applicable at the moment of intercourse.

(i) Should the female happen not to satisfy herself (in common language did not "come") then she is subject to headache or irritable-ness through the day and her parts may possibly keep running or wet. So this act must be a natural one and with an all-round fulfillment, because half-done acts will result in pain, strain and a burning sensation when you go to pass urine.

(j) After child delivery, it is not the best thing to have intercourse before three months because her vagina is very tender and sore. On most occasions, the female suffers but to avoid annoyance some unreasonable men will go to her even before the customary nine days are over and on most occasions the female groans in pain rather than enjoy herself.

The female parts expands for the child's head to pass and moreover, the hair on its head cuts and bruises the tender vaginal parts and she will constantly keep draining fluid all the time. Further, she may have to be under medications mostly locally, so as to avoid septic and thus blood poisoning. Intercourse, during the menstrual period, will result in an increase of the blood flow and it very often result in prolonging the cycle period.

From the medical science come many more professional teachings on the beginning of the human life, but in my work, it is uncalled for. They are not include and besides that, I am not that professional but more or less practical experiences, expressed in this work gained over the years as mentioned earlier. The clitoris has tissues which are filled with warm surging blood, during sexual excitement and it is very sensitive to the touch. This warmth provides an un-describe feeling and life to the male and his penis, plus extreme comfort to the woman on a slow entry into the vagina. In response, to this comfort the woman may kiss you, squeeze you tightly and bit you. Although, she means no harm, you may suffer however, slightly from her actions unknowing to her.

From the above, it is easy to understand excitement or arousal as a response. In woman is somewhat strange, for a while a handsome man plays a secondary role, in most occasions in sexual desires to a majority of women, it is the touches of the bodily contact of an erected penis, heightened her sexual desires. Arousal of sexual desires also varies with different women and at different times between one menstrual cycle to the other. Sometimes, peak periods of their desires may be climaxed mid-cycle, sometimes just before and during menstruation and very often, it is at this heated point that conception takes place.

When the vagina is in a high passion, it jumps, squeezing in contracts and releases at a reasonable pace and with the penis inside her, not only the female contracts, but extracts great satisfaction. The male also with a very slow upward and downward movement in her, he enjoys such a contraction and relaxed movements that he gets loss with excitement and therefore, expresses wonderful thoughts of enjoyments and satisfaction.

At an orgasm, the woman may make movements such as winning the hips, sideways and up and down inclusive of her buttocks or by jerking, trusting movements of her thighs and pelvic muscles. Some women may remain still, rigid and contracts her below parts during an orgasm. As a matter of fact some woman at different times her orgasm, may adopt herself to all of these varieties for there is pleasure in them all. Should she be aroused and not fully satisfied sexually by her husband, then she may go to the extreme and masturbate or as in commonly called self-relief.

CHAPTER 17

Impotence Guide

There are two streams of impotence in sexual life and they have great influence in the human life. I think every person; somewhere down the line do suffer from the outcome of these impacts.

The Physchological & Physical Impotence

The first, is based on thoughts the mind and the manner you think and act. It depends how deep seated is this mental agony and whether it could overcome by you or through simple advice from others by way of encouragement. If, it is more severely rooted, you should take treatment for a psychologist, who will give positive thought suggestions. The other is genuinely based on your physical health. In that, you become ill and weak. You will need the assistance of your physician, who will give you suitable medicine, such as vitamin B complex and other high potency drugs.

Your libido life force, emotional cravings, sexual urges, inclinations longings and desires, which are small parts of the total libido, has disappeared and cause you to become dis-interested in love-making. Also perhaps, in the female as a whole could be traced to these two causes. Some aggressive girls may take the first initiative, which may inject in you the kind of stimulant you are short of. Whatever the concoction of the female, trouble not yourself about it as long as it produces the desired results of an erection.

You will recall, that I said elsewhere, that if you have a health problem, to please consult your doctor immediately and despite the advice contained in this chapter, which is more or less based on preventive actions, that is, to see your doctor promptly.

My intention is to guide you in such a way as to actually prevent impotence, by taking the right types of food and this will improve sexual reality and satisfaction.

Many women are sexually starved and are known as "starved women". They want the full expression of their husband's love badly and they will not settle for a substitute, such as an electric blanket etc. They may be curious as to the real cause for their lack of sexual response and could turn to the wrong source, such as make-ups, attractive nightdresses and sensuous perfumes and may even use romantic manipulations. All of which happens to be a hopeless failure in the absence of the right approach and intentions.

Surprisingly, the loving and caring wife could very well brew the root cause in the kitchen. Your failure to follow up and sort out the cause will result in you seeking satisfaction and try to help solve the problem by your contribution to the solution that may very well be in the kitchen.

Food is the substance of life and our very make-up depends on its vitamins although, not the food itself, but the essential elements in the food and intakes varies according to age, size, health and occupation.

As I understand it, healthy glands are needed for a healthy sex life and general health as a whole. They are the mysterious chemical laboratories in the human body and they hold the secret of our sexual drive, plus other functionaries and they are the spark plugs, which triggers and stimulates our activities, both physical and mental.

The male sex hormone is called testosterone and the female is called estrogen. These play a dramatic role in the sex life. Glands are the fountain head of our sex display and this could be strengthening by vitamins and minerals in their right proportion intake. Some of the best source of vitamin B is wheat germ, brewer's yeast, liver, whole grains, nuts, beans, and brown rice and for the iodine help, is a good source rather than salt absorption of iodine. It could be taken together with wheat germ oil, about a glass of tomato juice with help the taste.

Located at the base of the brain, is a small but mighty master gland, called the pituitary glands. It is under the stimulus of this master gland, that the testes produce spermatozoa's and male sex hormones and the ovaries produce ova and female sex hormones. Malfunction of the pituitary gland, it is said, is the cause of impotence in males and premature menopause in the female.

Manly, strong and forceful, is the responsibility of zinc (mineral) supplement, which promotes the greatest degree of sex maturation. It is useful for fertility and virility. This trace mineral (zinc affects male performances and potentials. It is concentrated in bran and germ portion of cereal grains. Seeds have all the elements necessary to sustain a new life. Zinc rich foods are pumpkin-seeds, sunflower seeds; sesame seeds and all raw nuts also are herring, liver, mushroom, wheat germ, wheat bran, brewer's yeast, onions and maple syrup also fertile eggs.

Vitamin C: Prostatic fluid is extremely rich in vitamin C. It exists widely in most raw nuts and fruits; green salad leaves and shoots, tomatoes brussels sprouts, golden bantam corn and baked potatoes. Do you know that we pay less attention and value to the flesh of ripen fruit, which purpose is to protect the seed inside and this inside is the most valuable part. For it is the beginning of all life.

Vitamin E: This is often called the sex vitamin, inadequate consumption of same will cause decreases in both sex hormones and the pituitary hormone, which stimulates the sex glands and this vitamin also protects the sex glands and hormones form destruction by oxygen. It is suggested that one or two teaspoonful of wheat germ oil sprinkled with cereals or mixed with juices or milk should be taken. It will provide an adequate supply of vitamin E and so, too is fresh raw wheat.

Vitamin F (Fatty Acid): The essential fatty acid is useful to treat prostate disorders and menstrual disturbances. It is found in cold pressed unrefined vegetable oils, wheat germ oil, sunflower, safflower and Soya beans.

Iron: This extremely important mineral. Insufficient intake can cause tired blood, shortness of breath during exercise, headaches, poor complexion and little sex interest. It could be found in turnips, peaches, prunes, raisins, beans, peas and nuts.

Manganese: This is found in apricots, green vegetables, the outer coatings of nuts and grains, kelp, raw egg yolk and salt water fish. Combined potassium and manganese proved to be the magic password to open the bedroom door, particularly for those women suffering with housewife's syndrome, which is physical and emotional fatigue. The result of which is bedroom fatigue.

Potassium: sources are from beef, lamb, chicken, liver and turkey, almond nuts, walnuts and salted peanuts, green beans, peas lettuce, spinach, oranges, bananas, fresh fruits and seeds. Manganese is found tapping along with potassium and is found in dolomite, sesame, pumpkin, kelp, sunflower seed, sea salt, barley corn, Soya flower and cashew nuts for spatic acid asparagus, Soya beans, and sugar, beet, molasses.

Researchers and manufacturer have discovered and place on the market a few new patent medicines, claiming to assist impotent sufferers by restoring erection to them. In your confused state, you will be tempted to use the drugs secretly. However, beware, may I advise for it could be fatal. So, the best thing to do is to be in touch with your doctor, who will know exactly what action to be taken. Do not aggravate the situation worst, though your anxiety and concern.

These drugs, in most cases, are harmful to the users to take, so, take no risk, especially if you area heart sufferer. It is understandable, that to loose your sex drive or to be impotent, is indeed sad and frustrating to both parties and this may tempt you to blindly, rush in to a secret drive for help all by yourself.

Are you run-down and need strength and pep-up? Then use one teaspoonful or not exceeding ten drops of steel drops, one teaspoon of glucose, a pinch of salt and young coconut water at your discretion and see how you respond. It should give you vigor and vitality.

Both of these categories, are psychological and the first, will erase fear and build confidence giving a sound footing of love, which could encourage erection the male penis and the female clitoris, while, the second will encourage impotency by depression, and suppressed motivated sexual desires. If you suffer from the above, then, blame no one, neither yourself but go it all over again, following the given advice. It will soon be possible.

A type of impotency that affects, both male and female, is immature erection and ejaculations which are undesirable foes. With the male, the penis will not be stiff enough for a normal penetration and it will not give an enjoyable and satisfactory sexual fulfillment to either party, even if it is hand-forced into the vagina.

To many of you, it may be the first time you are learning that equally a female does have erection similar to a man. This is because, you do not actually see or feel her erect-able part, which is the clitoris, situated at the far upper, fold of the labia minors or commonly called the lips. It is the gently touches and play to this part, that gives the female erection and un-describe enjoyment to her. She then has an erection and falls just as a man.

It is now clear to the understanding that erection is caused by stimulation of sexual excitement, when the penis of the man and the clitoris of the woman will get rigid form the flush of blood that enters the blood vessels, thus, causing an expansion. This blood remains there and do not regain the normal circulation until the organ becomes flaccid, either from ejaculation or exhaustion.

Urologists, who are experts in male sexual organs, says that impotence is more or less a symptom, rather than an actual disease, for example, it is associated with patients of heart disease, high blood pressure, diabetes and prostate troubles and also drunkenness etc.

Although, I did not research, I am of the opinion that a large quantity of the world's population especially men do suffer from impotency of one kind or the other at some stage of their lives. As a matter of fact, all men will suffer from impotence, especially in old age.

CHAPTER 18

Abortion

Biblically, abortion I prohibited, maybe under normal conditions and when the expectant mother or parent just decided they do not want a baby. Because, it may have an adverse effect on the mother-to-be, plus shame in the family, especially if it is out of wedlock. Of course, this decision rests on the mother-to-be. There are known cases, where this is necessary to save a life of the intended mother, maybe, at this point it will be reported as legal and it must be done by a qualified doctor, who after examination of the patient, will advise accordingly. The lives of the mother and the baby are involved and it must be gone about cautiously.

I wrote this portion, so as to educate you on the dangers of abortion illegally. And to what extent, people may risk their lives in this exercise and so, that you may have a clear picture of what abortion is and you are not to agree or practice it, unless, it is exceptionally necessary and this is the be rightly done.

This advice becomes necessary because there are many people, who tried the "bush doctor or in other words we call Quack doctors" method and on some occasion, are successful. As I learnt some people insert into their wombs, foreign matters or objects, drugs bush-weed medicine, pressures on the abdomen, slips or heavy jerks. The skillful practice of inserting a drainage tube into the womb at any time between 1-2 months was afterwards spoken by those persons, who had undergone the ordeal.

Abortion is the detachment and expulsion from the pregnant womb of the product of conception. Fertilized ovum, embryo or fetus before twenty-eight weeks. Abortion occurs spontaneously, in many instances and it also can artificially induce. Indeed, induced abortions are either therapeutic—done under proper medical direction, to move a life and health of the mother or criminal abortion or commonly known as illegal abortion is a threat to a woman's life and health, whether self—induced or furtively performed by money-hungry racketeers.

Spontaneous abortion is called miscarriage and is accident prone of nature. Some women lose their potential babies repeatedly in the early months of pregnancy and this known as habitual abortion.

Natural type of abortion does occur and it is when the mother-to-be would lose her baby, sometimes habitually, without the induction of any drugs etc. The unfortunate cases should consult the doctor regularly and perhaps, will have her under observations from the beginning to the ending of her pregnancy period.

There are many cases, which do contribute to abortion, for example miscarriage that may or may not be willful act but by accident. The mother-to-be might have slip, a fall, a heavy jerk, lifting an unusual heavy weight or lack of proper care and attention to her-self when it should be.

To affect the cause some people may revert to herb medicine, medical drugs, seek doctor's help. Some may be too young to be a mother, may not wish to be burdened down with a child so early in life. Father does not want to own the child to be. Father may instruct to have an abortion because they may be afraid of parents and their abuses. Perhaps too poor and cannot afford to have a child. If unmarried, the child to-be may stand in the way of a future husband plus many, many more other causes.

Before twenty-eight weeks of pregnancy, the fetus from the womb is not able to survive outside the uterus, this expulsion if the fetus from the womb is abortion. In particular, the medical science and rightly so, being no doubt the competent authority, is doing research work to find more suitable solution in sex problems. That is how they come about with helpful prescription in this everyday demand.

Perhaps, as has been observed after a successful discovery, the researchers are too proud and thus slumber away in to a long trance only to be conscious again when an incurable pops up its head, then they will look for a solution. Of course, research is always and should be dissatisfied instruments hence, its proud greed into further in-depth, into will always be demanding.

Every man and woman has the right to be fearful and be concerned over sex failures which for my purpose, I classified or include impotence, sterility and abortion. If he or she does not, then they are not worth living and when they do they live for no purpose, therefore fail not to consult your doctor.

Seen in the everyday publications are advertisements of one kind or another of no mean influence for its readers which claim to be a new discovery to the much devastating destruction to the human race realizing that without reproduction the human race will vanish from the face of this planet.

Birth Control

I am obliged not to go in-dept, nor to give this topic any special attention because of the valuable information and materials, which are being released, dealing with birth control.

Further, the advice already given will serve as a genuine, natural and artificial guide.

CHAPTER 19

Child—Parent—Relationship

Having treated other areas in family life, through this work, I still felt that there was a missing link, which should be included. So I decided to include the infant period, because it is important for all sides.

I was really puzzled as to where I should commence this topic but, after some careful thoughts, I decided from this very wide range to begin for the purpose of this work from age two of the infant's life. This age group was chosen because from around this age, the child may start to walk or talk and so, develop natural intelligence through to seven years. Despite this book home training by parents will have to continue and for that matter, never cease through life.

The period of the human existence, which is the most important, for setting their foundation, and in rapid growth is the first few years after birth. It is also, the time of the greatest peril of life. Special effort and skilled in-puts to ensure a normal development of the child, is at this very beginning.

I cannot deal with this period before and after fertilization and the essential between that period to delivery. Suffice, to say in these brief comments. That the mother-to-be and the mother will have to take care of herself and also to follow the doctor's health advice and precautions.

Breast-feeding is the best for the newborn baby. However, during the first few days, the breast will contain no milk. Many young mothers do not want un-shaped breasts, so, they have a tendency to avoid nursing the baby and prefer to use artificial feeds. Your baby clinic adviser will provide you with a lot of baby care etc. information.

From about eight month the baby will start to observe objects but will not be sensible to distinguish them. Bright colored toys and interested objects within sight could be picked up. Teeth may start to appear and an attempt to mumble ma-ma, dada etc. will be observed careful watch for illness and prompt attending to your doctor is important, if baby is to survive.

By age two, the child could run and with a hand rail go up and down the stairs, turn door knob, open o shut a door, make attempt to scratch on paper or on the ground with a piece of stick or with pens or pencils. None of these will make any sense but they are all-important steps taken by the child. The toddler will imitate what he or she sees others do. Although not quite accurately, will get dress, undress and perhaps feed him or herself. None of which is done uniformly or properly.

By age three to four, the child will be ready for nursery school, to continue the task of being molded for the adult life. Here, the infant will run, jump and climb, string beads, draw crude pictures, enjoy and play with toys and listen to short stories, songs and nursery rhymes and would make great efforts to repeat what so ever you will teach him or her. He or she is ready now on for a lot of creative activities and develops a very high sense of infant imaginations, even the expectation of parents. He will, with delight describe his achievements to you, tell of the games he played with others and make up stories by himself, enough to your understanding and with you help. You will boost the child brain, which in a kind of a way is actually, preparing the child for his entire future.

You may be surprised to learn, that the greatest and smartest professor that you could think about started in this very same small way, from the lowest class at school, number one to ten and the alphabet A to Z. The rest of his knowledge through university was a process of developing from this tiny and what appears to be unimportant beginning. He will return from nursery school with a lot of ideas gained from his other school mates and this will result in lots of questions from the toddler's inquisitive mind.

At this point, you will have, not only to be patiently entertain the child, but to also encourage him or her to come up with more questions. Do not cut short the child nor railroad their ideas. Do not shout or scream on him or her because they are asking too many questions or that the questions are wrong. In time they will develop themselves to ask their entire question the correct way. Don't even tell him or her that the questions are wrong but rather show him or her the right way in a loving manner and you will be surprised of the response. Too often, parents waste time trying to correct a child with the negative, rather than the positive language and this cause the child to retain more wrong than right.

Thus, childhood is the period in the human life that begins at infancy and is ended with physical maturity, so they cannot avoid mistakes as a toddler and even repeat the very wrong over and over again. Parents have to adopt ways and means by carefully observing and experimenting to arrive at a suitable system. I guess you may dismiss this idea by saying that parents are too busy to be observant and help the child, who, is in dire need at this early point in their life.

It is by trial and errors, that we can learn things, which of course, never cease all through our lives and more is responsible for what we are today. The child is no exception to this true paragon.

All of us are born with certain capabilities to learn, some children develop at their own rate in their own way and time. Here is a typical example of our tongue as I understand it, the sensitivity of the tongue is said that he front part of tongue gives tasting to sweet, the back taste bitter while the sides or edges gives taste to salty things. While the vision senses starts only with light and darkness then followed by distinguishing colors such as red and green, then yellow and blue.

In order to learn you will have to teach the child along these lines with these objects and so build their attention and interest. There are many interesting theories on the methods and processes of teaching and learning. However, none of them are yet entirely satisfactory and could give full explanation of what is called the best methods of learning.

The young child will always want to talk about what he or she learnt with someone, the matter becomes more firmed on the mind. You will have to encourage this sort of dialogue as parents and to also get in touch with the school teacher, who will give you an update on his or her progress with in the guidelines of school training. The coordination will be very helpful and effective for the benefit of the child.

There is individual difference in learning between children. Some are able to learn almost anything easily and to retain it without difficulties. While others make very little learning progress and to forget everything very quickly. This causes both parents and child to be despondent and frustrated, however, this must not be for, and here are many causes where exceptionally weak children turn to be clever professors. This causes the teachers to say that they do not believe in children being called dunce or illiterate.

The child build on the early training that he had in the beginning and as parents, you greatly influence the young child by your home behavior and life styles. This coordination is very effective to the child and you shall bring in the sheaves with joy, satisfaction and contentment and to say, "The job is well done."

Very often, when the child happened to err both the mother and or the father would scold the child as the circumstances do warrant. This is the right approach when it comes to correcting the child.

Parents must display equality and impartiality towards their children and at the same time children must not allowed to have their own way. You are to be artful and skillful in our methods when dealing with explosive situations. A level head with calmness could dispel much of the anxieties and restore things back to order to the joy of all sides.

I now bring to your attention a few common ailments, which the parents could manage at home, but this does not rule out the doctor according to the severity of the case. I will therefore, deal with only those common and regular visitors, which could be successfully treated at home.

(1)   The Common Cold: Common cold with influenza and fever.
Treatment: when this is actually on, the infant could be covered with a blanket, leaving out the face and about half an hour, the child would have perspired enough for

the covering to be removed. Then the child is to be dried and given other clothes and the recovery from fever, would be instant and relief would be had for the other attackers. While, on the treatment exercise you will have to take a close look at the child for any signs and if so, promptly remove all coverings immediately.

(2)   Headaches: Take you two fingers or thumb and place them at the temple area or where ever the pain is felt. Apply pressure while at the same time you are rubbing downwards at the forehead going back-wards, repeat this two or three times. The pain will be gone.

(3)   Minor eye problems: You must make KAAJAR with oil but with clarifies butter (ghee). Place ghee on an ordinary spoon and place same over a burning lamp that is giving off soot, which will be trapped by the ghee in the spoon. Place this collection around the eyelid at the eyebrow and leave overnight.

(4)   For headache: just sap some ghee on the hand, which will moisten and keep head cool and the pain, will go away.

(5)   Belle pain caused by gas: Take one tablespoon full Bay rum with salt it will work wonders.

(6)   To keep healthy, use a juicy fruit a day which will give you a bowel movement a day not forgetting a balanced diet plus physical exercise and rest are all important contributions for a good health.

(7)   If your eyes are running, water and painful and sticking, especially when the sun is setting, go to an experienced person who knows how to remove the bad hairs or (hog-hairs).

(9)   Aloe-Juice: when this is place on an affected part it will heal e.g. Burns, minor skin irritation, rashes etc. scrape off aloe skin and place it on bruises etc. it will soften and moisten your skin.

(10)   Vaginal itching: wash same with like warm water mixed with aloe juice.

(11)   Dry leathery skin: if you look older than you are, then you should apply papaw mixed with aloe and olive oil

and a few drops of lime juice, whip to a cream and place on face or other parts of the body.

(12) For shiny and smooth hair: wash hair with aloe shampoo.

(13) For dandruff: wash hair with ochro leaves and if hair is weak, use ironweed boiled and cool off.

(14) Garlic eaten raw or mixed in Soya bean oil is good for foul breath and a long and healthy life. Chew a few fleg with chlorophyll (could be had from green tops of plants) daily.

(15) Bee pollen: known as bee bread is a wonderful food you can eat.

(16) Royal jelly: this is made by bees as food for the queen, could be your food also, so as to grow strong and live long, with honey it is all round food, use it freely. It can be used also for eye drops.

(17) Onions goes with garlic provides vitamins, minerals and other nutrients. Use it fresh. It can also ease pain caused from stings, just cut and place on an affected part.

(18) To throw of fat and weight, use grapefruit every day.

(19) For blood pressure (high) use grapefruit and molasses.

(20) Lower cholesterol:, This is responsible for high blood pressure, then use abundantly avocado, peanut and other oily vegetables. Use papaw and banana for a bowel movement.

CHAPTER 20

The Home—A Red Chapter

A s I searched the mind and with deep reflections, I consider to bring this chapter into my book. I think, for it to be left out would result as cause an incomplete book presented to you. I begin in this book with love, joy and happiness that culminated with togetherness, that is in marriage and I wish to add to this work by bringing to your attention and at the same time to warn you of some pit-falls and dangers of a BROKEN Home. In short, separation of that once lovely togetherness, this started when you both first met.

Before you both think of separating, why not look back to those early days, when you started your love affairs. What you said then and the way you both acted is filled with a lot of self-guidelines and corrections, for both parties. So, much so, that it was through that great love, you were brought together.

When there is imminent danger through misunderstanding, in a broken home, why not look right back to the courtship days, which are filled with an abundance of valuable materials to avoid a broken home. Advise, from other people at such a trying time are useful and had proven helpful but, the best of all advice, which is truly being ignored, is found in your courtship volume. Go to it and implement those skillful arts over and over again as often as you can and everything there is a misunderstanding in the home should wisdom prevail, you will find the courtship magic is the best and is better than all the rest of advice. Why suffer, when you have all the required ingredients, found in your early days and first love. Turn to it, I say give it an honest trial and allow it to work in your heart that you will succeed. Do not put on the negative.

To part, no matter how, when or what is the cause, is always sad, particularly if you have been blessed with children. There bound to be moments of regrets and should you permit separation to supercede your deep seated love for each other and the children, and to cause it to bring about a broken home? Then there is nothing calls love.

Above all causes (some of which will be mentioned later on), absence of God in the heart, and this is the greatest and chief obstacle to all broken homes, especially, when the parties do not have a fleshly heart, but they both put on a heart of stone. Only, Only, then forgiveness for shortcomings on both sides cannot find a resting-place.

In the human heart, there is the temple of God and a workshop for the devil, so the result is no turning back, but ends in miserable situation of separation. I cannot bring to your attention all the problems and solutions, this I think is somewhat impossible, by my attention and attempt to enlighten you along this path, quite briefly, should suffice to assist you as you tumble along life's journey, where you will gather your own experiences.

It was the most joyful moment when wedding bells sounded at full blast, for the couple in love and this goes on around the world. Yet, the sad moment await the determination and penetrates to inflict their wounds upon some lovers. For too often, this tragedy enters the home in various disguises from of a menace society. Homes are broken and shattered like broken glass and families are separated. Thus divorce is on the increase.

I do not pretend by trying to tell you, that this book is the cure-all or will end or remedy divorce, but at least, if the advice given, is adhere to, it will assist to curb and be helpful to minimize disputes between two out-raged parties and reduce the increase on divorce plus perhaps, reunite the love ones and they would not go over the precipice and join the already crowded broken-homes in lamentation, whether civilized or uncivilized, we are all the very root and the system of togetherness of the populated world.

A home is more than just four walls, a roof, internal walls and furniture. Is indeed beyond that, for it is a family living together happily. In that super-structure, until death do us part. There is no room in that mansion for divorce or a broken home or even disputes and sad faces.

Much depends on a woman to make her marriage work successful; of course, she is to be a good wife, helpmate to her husband and ever-loving mother and keeper at home. Please, avoid being the boss! Take heed, as to how far you could push your husband. Do not go beyond, especially, when you see sign of annoyance. You could always try to put over your point another day, when the atmosphere is cooler and you would be better entertained.

Let us look at some of the problems, children or mechanics that may be responsible in some way or the other to put their spanners to work, in dismantling the wedded home and causes the home to be broken and ends in divorce—adultery unfaithfulness, covetousness, drunkenness, stealing, third-party type of company, busy-body, criminal background, unevenly yoked, health and maybe planetary disagreements, laziness, bareness, impotence, suspicion, distrust, building etc. none of these will ever take care of the good side in a home.

I wish to classify the home under three broad-based un-escapable headings:

1. A happy home.
2. A miserable home, plagued with ups and downs and unquenched quarrels most of the time.
3. A broken home, separation, hatred etc. over-power the sweet and joyful love which cause not only the first togetherness, but the continued togetherness until both parties give way to the ugly menace, which cause an evil spell and a dark gulf which is built up between the once sun shine of love.

Beware, for separation in most occasions, for those, except in a few isolated cases, cause great grief, pain and sufferings. It is said that "house worries" is the worst type of worries, further, to this all sorts of eye-pass and advantages will be fall the wife and children, especially a girl-child to come from would-be sympathizers. Who would show up to render help and would seek from you the woman, sexual intercourse as a means of re-dress.

A second husband, very rarely live up to his promised paradise to you. You may seldom flourished or enjoy his companion-ship for long and you may very well have to abide under all the adverse conditions. Perhaps, worst than you first marriage because you would not want, or be ashamed to have a second or third or more separation. All in all, it was better if not for yourself but for the children's sake to have abide with first husband and if you are wise enough, you can influence your husband and cause your marriage to last to the end of your days.

Should you, this wife prefer to choose the RED ROAD, then you being the weaker vessel, will have to live the balance of your life in curse and insults, because at the slightest misunderstanding between yourself and the new husband, he will bring unpleasant remarks to you and keep referring to your former husband, you will vehemently rebute because this would not meet your taste. Time and time again, these remarks will prop up its ugly head and so, the home will gradually loose peace and respect for each other. Affection, will also deteriorate and possibly, completely absent and the stage will be reached where it could no longer be tolerated by either party and this could be followed by nothing more but a broken home.

It was brought out, that many divorce were due to lack of a little understanding and the application of a little patience and tolerance. Looking back, it could be seen that the major disaster had started from foolishness, and instead of subsiding, it escalated to the point of no turning back (broken eggs), but erupts to a daily nagging feature, which backfire in SEPERATION.

At the beginning, all had seen the rising of a bright horizon and a splendid and happy future and when separation drives a wedge between the couples, it is not only broken-home, but a broken, sad and miserable heart, filled with a lot of regrets and thoughts, to cause a nervous breakdown. you will have to begin life's journey anew, with care to avoid the evil repeating itself, but somehow, unknowing, you get entangled again and the result in frustration. Feeling, life is not worth living. Please, decide!. It does not work and your problems do not end. Hold on, someone, anybody good and kind to help is still out there.

As I write this chapter, with the touches of sadness from a broken home, I am embraced with feverish thrills of the unbearable sufferings one will have you endure at the hands of a broker home. Besides, the personal infliction's you will have to face up to the ridicule, bad remarks indecent slangs and the many more adverse sayings form the public. Added to this, mournful plight is when a sledgehammer strikes away from within, you heart.

All marriages started out with high hopes for betterment. Hence do not let yours be a tug-o-war, why should you two grown up lovers, hurt each other of much and so far? Do not permit a thin unseen wall of stubbornness to be the veil between two matured, sincere lovers with that first brilliant horizon of dazzling golden rays.

Sex rationing, without approval and maliciousness, will surely anger both persons and it must be recalled, that both parties to have a breaking (unbearable) point when both partners could recognize that each was wrong to each other and a matters were taken too far. Please drop the bomb of forgiveness with love and with open arms, receive what belongs to you and say "I am sorry", "I love you" and that will do the trick and open the way for the cooler step to be taken, where the passion will be of a different kind.

You do not truly want a breakup, nor want to lose your loved one. Then, look to your loved one with love and not hatred and passion. See in your loved one the love and beauties of beauty blossom just in front of your eyes, why suffer unnecessary pain and anguish? Instead of the reward of kindness and love and so eat of the fruit of your labor, drink and eat form the fountain. Enjoy it, for it is yours to take. The cake is already out so eat gluttony to your and her fill.

Marriage is not a bed of roses; it has its taste of pleasure and displeasure and in most cases, the second thoughts of the children, binds the vows and keeps the fire kindled into reunion.

Men is liken to the tide. One day up (washing tide) and the other time down (falling tide). Sometimes, the river is very calm not even a ripple to be seen, while other times mountains waves could be seen. After a calm not even comes a storm and these are exactly, the reality and experiences of life. It will happen with the married, as well as the unmarried. One must therefore be prepared for these eventualities in life and make the best out of it because "if yo mek yo bed haad yo mus lie pan it" if yo buy yo kalico, yo mus wear am". Life then is what you make it, and not what you want to make it, or is it the imagination or wishes that you have within you.,

Obviously to say farewell to a home that you worked hard to build, needs a lion's heart, because it tears the inside and the blows so heavy, that it burst the liver in two. I have talked to many husbands and wives who had gone through the ordeal of a broken home and they all expressed regrets that it had to be so and they felt that had they known any better, or had been any wiser before, the lesson they learnt from the Broken Home, that may not have had to happen.

I hope, with the knowledge disclosed in this work, you will never be caught in that vicious act of a broker home. How would you feel, should you see another person ill-treating the person you once loved dearly and worst of all to see your dearly children suffers at the hands of a step-father and as very often happens, your daughter is to be pregnant for her step father, or that she had gone astray for the want of a father's protection and providence. Surely, you cannot easily live with the shame but too late, would be the cry, because you cannot right what has already gone wrong. The best thing to do is don't let it happen at all.

Stop your broker home situation, before it happens and no doubt to break you down personally and is in some occasion beyond repairs. I urge you, and I am making a special appeal to both parties that should a broken home materially appear, both of you should go out of your way to make the marriage last and to be a happy one. Absolutely, modern day teaching tells us that if it cannot work then let it go . . . . but at what price? This is not only pleasing you but to the children also, who would walk the road very proud and with a lifted head and maybe use your union as an example in their life pattern. "a happy and lasting togetherness—no broken home for you

Women, are mostly the aggressive ones, filled with passion and are overtaken with ignorance and blindness, which cause them not to keep their mouth shut and when the husband would have said one word, the wife, like a machine gun shooting out loud words, which are indeed very stinging and when he cannot keep pace with the words then he ignores the saying "mouth and mouth gat story han na business". He, being the stronger one will turn to his hands for rescue but there are some husbands, who will leave the home and go for a walk to cool off.

Should you, the wife stay quiet and I urge you, try it, you will find the husbands will quickly end the quarrel. Did you ever stop and consider that both of you have loosed out because nothing can replace what have gone out of both of you in the race dispute.

I learnt from old people sayings, "a little out of sight test the strength of love, and maybe, a good antidote, if things get too hot and this should never be, then, take a few days holidays, but whether, your vacation leave will be approved? Is another story and if it should, then go to some and relative some distance away where you could be secluded from the husband" sight. Do not however, be away for too long, less both parties should get accustomed to do without each other and this will contribute to greater problems. Just a few days absence will put both of you to the anxiety pitch and climax of missing each other and the urge to be back together in each other's arms. At this point, you must not stifle or suppress your love demands, but to quickly return home.

There is no home without minor or petty differences or misunderstandings, but whatever the cause, it must not cause the love candle to grow chill or to go out because it is not easy to forget. I want nobody else as my only possession as long as there is life, which means everything to me. This should be echoing loud and clear to the burning heart fill with love. If you put this Macedonian call aside, you will have a broken home. Just give me your heart of love and we will never part, this is a grand appeal and a striking promise indeed.

A broken home, will cause you to be unstable like a bee and to go from flower to flower in search of food and nectar and you will sooner or later become exhausted and fade away, also face the risk of getting disease. If you do not want to get drowned in the ocean of problems, or get loss in a wilderness of worries, where you may look at all the natural beauties but still cannot make use of them then, for peace and love sake, you are to be forgiving and loving. You should be adjustable and adaptable to circumstances and you should be flexible and by so doing, neither parties will hear and answer the call of "separation" neither separation will not hang on, nor lurk around you but will run away in shame. While, on the other hand, should you respond? Then, shame will strike you with a heavy and unbearable blow and that scar will always remain.

Does my message touch your heart? If it has then, prevention is better than cure and persuasion and constant dripping of kind words will wear away the stony heart. Be gentle as a dove, and let your voice be as the nightingale in the night and like a lark in the day. Your smiles, attractive and charming as magic, your touches gentle, thrilling and soothing as velvet and your satisfaction be as long draught of saccharine and perfumed with the fragrance of flowers. All of which, will make a great impact upon an unforgettable heart which is not from within a beast, but a human which do have the power to reason and the gift of senses and not instinct as found in a dumb beast which will stimulate forgiveness.

A woman is always a light in the home and without her, Satan dwells therein, it becomes a home of darkness. Hence, go of that useful light she will be a "lamp unto your feet and a light unto your path". Hopefully, you will not fall. Hence, there is no opportunity for the stranger known as Separation which is rapping at the door of your home to gain entry and should it be successful, then it will leave behind on its parting Mr. Hard time, Dilemma and Woeful Predicament which joins you to the company of a broken home and a broken heart.

Here is a story, dealing with a separation between and husband and wife. The husband and wife had a great dispute and decided to separate. As a result he instructed his wife how to share up the property with everything that he owned must be shared between his children this exercise, went quite smoothly, because the wife was pleased with the sharing up also. She was quite cool and level headed and arrived at a wise move, when she said to her husband that it was her turn to share the rest of the property that he had left out. They both agreed, but he was truly surprised because he thought that he had made a good job of the sharing and truly, nothing was left out.

He was extremely anxious to hear what the wife had to say and she, very cleverly did as if she was searching as to what to say and suddenly, she dropped the bombshell, she lifted her dress and showed her nude self and kept patting her vagina and asking her husband to whom must she share her estate. On seeing this husband could not resist the temptation and his jealously was sudden and severe, that he jumped up and start making love and amend matters and lived happily ever after.

These are the magic charms, you the woman have, what of you? Which road will you take, this man could not have bear to live and hear that another man would make use of his wife and children's mother.

A wicked and unreasonable wife will keep repeating to her husband his past mistakes. Some wives take it a pleasure to do this, coupled with abuse, frame-ups, and accusations etc. that was never done. Of course, their behavior is mostly based on ignorance or uncontrolled passion. What aroused these actions does not matter to her because the object is as long as she gets to blow off herself. She did not care of the consequences that follow. Whom, she hurts or to what extent are the damages. In her quiet moments, after she normally feels guilty and sorry for her behavior later.

Surprisingly, however, this action will keep repeating itself; because no genuine lesson is ever learnt from these past mistakes. To ease the tension, some men would lock up their wife in room and go away with the keys, only to return as early as he averages things have abated. Some men are also guilty of these behaviors, both parties will have to take control of themselves and make the necessary requirements adjustable.

The shifting spanner, commonly called crescent, is a wonderful example and ideal lesson for all of us. You may wonder how it is possible. Well, the shifting spanner could adjust yourself to suit the prevailing circumstances and then adjust by the mechanic to fit screws. Similarly, both will be overtaken with love and peace, which will promptly follow. You may not doubt have a lack of self-knowledge that manipulated the young couple towards love, peace and the extraction of that wonderful pleasure that could be had from each other. Thus, welding the world as a whole.

In a problem infested home, remember that your courtship vocabulary or lovemaking dictionary have abundant of healing materials. You must make use of your vehicles of your acetylene torch and arc-welding plant, to seal the breach and is to bring your dispute to an end.

To you married people, I wish to say to you, a hearty and sincere welcome to this most ancient building which is to be your future dwelling house and must be found from the loveliest decorative materials to build your home. Let me take this opportunity to introduce you to this new accommodation and to show you around the pleasant, wonderful beautiful and most exciting architectural layout which is to be for your future happiness.

As we enter herein, which is the living room; in this part of the building, you will put on your boxing gloves, for it is your parliament and place of argument, mostly unsettled. Next, to follow is the appetizing preparation ground known as the kitchen where you will get your fingers burn and you will quickly place your fingers in the cooler. You may want to ask what or where is the cooler? Well, the cooler is let us say, we are playing cricket and the ball happens to pound your fingers while batting. You will hear shouts from the pavilion spectators, to put he injured fingers in the cooler. The cooler is now, between the legs.

Again, let us pay a visit to the last section of the building, which is your bedroom and this is your cooler or freezer. This is the point, where all your problems and disputes or misunderstandings that arose elsewhere, in the living room and kitchen are to bring to an end and fully settled through the cooler system. It is said, that you must not allow the sun to set on your wrath and if you truly love each other, then the freezer or cooler is good enough to cool your temper down and for you to turn a new page.

Always remember what GOD has joined together, no man must put asunder. Neither you, nor anybody else is to cause or put a separation between you and your spouse. It must take two to cause a problem and so too, it takes two to make peace or end the problem.

In love, there is no room for distrust. So seek yours what maybe with simplicity of heart because wisdom will not enter now dwell in the malicious soul. The good spirit of discipline with righteousness will flee the deceitful, for they are without understanding. However, you are urged to listen to the voice of knowledge and vengeance will pass by and no wicked deeds will ever manifest themselves.

Beware, for the jealous ear hears all things and nonsense, and the noise of assuming is not hid. These are unprofitable, therefore, refrain yourself from back biting. Remember that it is the heart through the mouth by the tongue, which belies what slay you. Later a choice is like crowning yourself with roses that withered and as flowers of the spring pass you by speedily and you will fail to contribute to the pleasure of the senses. By then your strength will be feeble and worth nothing. Should you put your trust in your faithful lover, then you shall understand the truth and your fateful love shall abide until the end of time.

To have an unsuitable partner, means having an imperfect branch with dishonor and this shall be broken off, their fruit unprofitable not ripe to eat nor is meet for anything. Discipline, is love in reality, so keeping the instruction and paying heed to the head of the home will keep away corruption.

CHAPTER 21

Divorce—A Dim Light Shines

D ivorce or not to divorce? Please read on for the answer but first let me give you the meaning of this popular word, which is used by increasing quantities in today's world. Divorce—in law this is a legal dissolution of the bonds of matrimony or the formal separation of husband and wife by a court of the land. Dissolution: the breaking up or ending of a legal relationship such as partnership or marriage. It is a decree of dissolution of a marriage, granted by a high court as proof of a matrimonial offence by either party e.g. adultery, desertion, cruelty or curable unsoundness of mind for the five years before the petition or that a husband has been guilty of rape, sodomy etc. Let me be open-minded on the above questions, whether to divorce or not to divorce?

(a) I would like for no one to get divorce and
(b) Yes, one should be divorce if it so warrants and is the only way out.

It is not my intention through this book or any other medium to stop divorce or separation of a couple because it is impossible for me to do so, but rather I seek to minimize it to the best to my mortal ability in this human world. However, it is my candid couple, adheres to the advice herein given; surely, there can be no divorce in the human race. One must comply with these suggestions to the latter and in better spirit and if this is done, it will be seen that truly, there will be no cause for a divorce or it can be avoided.

I am however, conscious that there will be people who will fail to stick closely or strictly to what is written. A separation is only due to the fact that you are personally guilty of disregarding the given advice and should you honor that contents of this book in the breach, what more could you expect? Both parties are urged to cooperate and comply with all that is written and if you do, there will be no room for a divorce or regrets but you will bid farewell and rebuke it to leave your home in peace, rather in pieces. My observation are that, divorce will only penetrate and find lodging, where there is a broken home, a broken heart and broken love and cooperation is lacking. It is a single street with a two lane, one for the husband and the other for the wife and both have to comply with the rule of the traffic, if a collision is to be avoided. However, although one knows the rules of this marriage game, yet both parties will breach them and at this point, cause a fatality much to the displeasure of the survivor.

In the common society of today and far and wide, there have been frequent—divorce and separation for when both parties think that way, I wish to advice not to act but just think of it both of you. Don't do anything. I suggest, just think about it over and over, harder and harder. Before long, both of you will no doubt, get all and fed up about the whole idea. Both of you are sensitive people and the amount of disclosure from both of you will certainly kill you emotionally and finally from both of you there will be desperate attempt to save the marriage. You will find the turning point much earlier that you think.

The mistakes is that both parties thought that marriage is a fifty-fifty proposition, but it is not, rather you must think and act this way and regard it as a seventy-five seventy-five bargain, that is, each going over that fifty-fifty mark. Should each person strive for the seventy-five percentages, that extra percent mark, then you will pass with credit and not a failure.

Divorce is very often followed by several embarrassing demands, which are unavoidable and besides the embarrassment in a court of law. It is followed by the society. As a result, both parties and children if any, suffers a mental and physical strain and stress, which have to be a constraint to live with for a long time in the future, even if you find another partner. In a case of the nature, the woman will feel the brunt of society and no doubt also from another husband if, she do remarry or even have a common law husband.

If two persons, as husband and wife cannot get along happily in life, the best thing to do, is to separate honorably. However, this book contains enough good information which will build up love and thus, avoid a separation. While, human will remain human beings, their actions could very well be those of a lower beast or cruel animal which could not be tolerated and it is this behavior that spurs the weaker partner to seek a divorce.

Did you ever stop to consider where your problem lies? It is found in the word misunderstanding (the prefix mis—wrongly) therefore, when there is a mis-understanding in the home, it simply means that one of you wrongly understands the matter in question and that only right or best thing to do is, to set it aside immediately. It must not be entertained less it will foolishly be the destructive agent in your life. Whereas if you destroy it understandingly (intelligent) will fill the vacancy and all things will quickly settled.

At a marriage, it is a simple single agreement by two parties and two hearts of love, laid upon one alter, which is glowing with fire of decisive love, to take each other as a life partner. While, at a divorce forum, a long drawn out method is put in the place with great embarrassment and uncalled for, exposures have to be undergone in the presence of a Judge in the Court of Law. It is here the woman in most cases, through her attorney wants to win the divorce proceedings and similarly, the man also wants to win the divorce case. As to avoid the financial involvement, will do great battle, with a lot of denials and untruth will surface as they are extracted through the trials, which goes on for a long period.

My opinion, a quick and simple divorce, is based on this suggestion that the interested parties desirous of a divorce, should appear before a marriage officer with their presentations of a petition or request for a divorce and both parties sign the divorce certificate as they did at the marriage, which will go through the normal proceedings by the competent authorities. The other portion of the matter dealing with a reward, or compensation (alimony) if cannot be agreed on and settled by the marriage officer, could be referred to the court for appropriate actions.

It is to be clearly understood, that no matter, what meaningful efforts you make, if your life partner do not cooperate by doing his or her part, success can never achieved. It is only from reality, you can truly experience which are probably your own or, they are based on others.

This work has brought out both streams. That is why it is a valuable document, which perhaps could bring about a new life standard. Something, we all need. We must work towards it, if we help ourselves there is a possibility of us receiving help.

Man is deeply involved in the use of natural environment and political change he is not static but keeps pace with modification in a continually changing society, resulting in a desperate search for a suitable avenue, with solution to meet these challenges by a chosen one. The woman should be no doubt the most beautiful sight before the man and so too, a man is the choicest and boldest and noblest for the woman. Both people for each other. Happiness is the linking for each other. For only by sharing life together, could a husband and wife taste for each other the richest joys. Separation can in no way offer this splendid unforgettable opportunity nor, under no circumstances, could either party go it alone.

You are to preserve unity, at all times and at all cost. The pair must keep confidence and mutual trust. Private matters at all times must be kept within the walls of the home as a secret, for it belongs only to the two of you. Misunderstandings are to be a priority, to be given urgent attention and be settled once and all, without the dangerous, vain repetitions, commonly indulged in by all of us. Let love prevail and be corner stone and temper—cooler if there is a quarrel. Only when love dies, hatred takes over and fills the vacancy.

As you read this book, you may want to conclude, that with all the knowledge, experiences and solutions given, that I had a life in "paradise" but it is not so. As a matter of fact, it is because of the several problems I decided to write this book, which will assist the others to avoid the unfortunate situations.

My desires, is not to hand out to you food for thoughts, which is the old sayings, but rather, to present to you my own founded expressions of giving thoughts for food, which have to be assimilated by both husband and wife and brought out in practice, if a divorce is to avoided.

To walk the path of divorce, where is a very dim light shines, will certainly cause you to stumble because visibility will be limited. Can this book be looked upon as words which are a lamp unto your feet and a bright light to your path, which will prevent you from stumping your feet and cause you not to fall and receive a heavy blow?

"You break up your love, you can and must build it back" all that is needed, is love, mercy, kindness, compassion and forgiveness but if you lack love, mercy, kindness and compassion then you will never practice forgiveness.

The quarrels, separation, expensive divorce and hatred, could be avoided or bought to an end with a simple word of unity just "forgive" and this will work miracle if you truly love each other. This cost, not a penny but sense and humbleness as found in a little child. The energy you use to break and destroy your home, please use the same energy to rebuild it. Don't be arrogant and hasty. Leave what you are doing immediately and meaningfully, forgive your spouse. Is this very hard to do? I don't think it is, rather it is very simple and maybe that is why it is being over looked and do not find a place in your heart.

SHIPWRECK

Let me introduce you to one of the most tantalizing and controversial topic that spans the marriage life. Some may be carefree, while others are somewhat concerned. It must be clearly understood because you may have learnt or seen of this matter which I refer to as BITTER-SWEET. Therefore, do pray with a wise head that you never have to cross that bridge of sorrow and climb the mountain of wreckage. No matter how pressing is your desire and satisfying the appetite towards ruining each other. You must free yourself from the scornful fetters and don't let them deprive you of a prosperous voyage.

The things that cause the wreckage are truly great antagonists, found where ever you go. Therefore, be on the alert and do not slip but follow the honorable company and have all fraudulent arrangement that will prejudice each other. Be settled and be back on friendly and loving, enjoyable terms and do not let it be your fault on that destruction.

This is a challenge on this great tournament, do not journey in or swaggering, rakish, dissipated ship and be at extremely with equal animosity and also use the fatal sword. Be decently furnished and shout joyfully that you won the barriers, common among human life, such as infected with passion, envy, avarice, despair, superstition, inclusive of love for the like cares.

A manageable garden will be spoken of its beauty, its bright and diversities of color and flowers, inclusive of the fragrances by which it fumigates the area in a mingle suspense of the surrounding air. From this, it is not a funeral and no cause for mourning and wearing of a black band with hands on the head or sticks to the jaw. You have to be a clever pilot to navigate your ship on the high seas. Similarly, marriage lie symbolically, could be compared to that of a sailing vessel, steered and maintained. Do you find a wife different from this? Let us examine this question more carefully.

Is you ship, whether courtship or marriage has been a wreck or sunken? Then, every effort of patience, skillfulness and care in handling the salvaging operation as input are to be no dream any longer. This period demands a change of attitude and a forgiving spirit by both parties. It is a new life and system of overlooking what has been the past, sweetly in a spirit of Love.

Dazzle the eyes, stirs the senses so it is that man or woman towards one another does use deceitfulness to charm either one and combines with natural beauty with the use of make ups are only vain outlook and these are all fakes.

I therefore do not stand in the way of your beauty power or popularity, but rather my critics are based on the mis-uses of these gifts, which are the root of the shipwreck. A ship sailing whether by wind or power driven, here I try to speak of a man or a woman under legal marriage or common law living together as husband and wife could suffer wreckage by:

(1) A break down in power to control each other.
(2) The ship becomes uncontrollable, due to failure of steering equipment and rudder.

(3) Bad management at sea or to the vessel itself by poor maintenance.
(4) To run a-ground at dangerous point.
(5) To dash against rocks etc. and spring a leak from heavy damages.
(6) Failure to have repair equipment's is at hand.
(7) Communication for assistance.

Sailing thought a strait is liken to a love affair. Here, two are connected and that you are also journeying thought life's path with the adjustment that you see around you and wish to adopt. It is known fact, that approximately 90% of the present day population in your area, will intervene at a love wreckage, not to amend matters, but to tell you to leave the man or woman as the case may be and that another better one is out there waiting for you. They may even go as far as to show you the way and assist you to affect the wreckage.

Remember, in salvaging the wrecked ship not only all necessary efforts are to be used but you first have to think well, with no confusion or excitement. Also, to examine all advice given, inclusive of good tools and then you will be in a position to approach the wreckage rightly.

The object here is to just impress upon you that you have to get prepared and equip yourself and then tackle your wreckage intelligently.

I place for your information and guidance, the following, which are briefly touched in this work and I leave you to select that which concerns you and would need your correction. As given below an explanation of the three most destructive words created from one.

(1) Wreck: These cover and include disabling or destruction or ruin of a ship, train, railway, building, industry and people etc.
(2) Wreckage: Being driven ashore, dashed against rocks founded by stress of weather or the like. Goods etc. cast ashore of a shipwreck disaster of navigation.
(3) Wrecker: Poor health, badly damaged, to tear down, to dismantle, to bring to ruin of disaster, to overthrow, thwart, defeat.

Remains of materials and something that has been wrecked: a person or thing in addition one who causes ruin, obstruction or disruption of any kind. In a broad sense, wreckage would not refer only to those causes where a husband and wife are separated. Separated by injury one another in so many ways and either one leave the marital home and love and take monetary passion which is responsible for all that follows. If it is a common law living together it also includes those causes where, although both parties are living under one roof, you will find that they are not speaking to each other nor, do they attend and serve each other, also they do not wash, cook nor dwell together.

Can a radiant BRIDE, with all her splendor and beauty, who had walked down the aisle or marriage path to pledge herself, her heart and life to the one and only one she chooses to be in union with thought marriage, could be sunken as a wreckage and permitted to remain below that dept or water? Can you afford the luxurious wastage, having toiled so hard to provide the best or that wedded moment? In that pledge was loyalty, honesty and sincerity, which are the best out of any human and their all.

Surely, it is not possible to allow that bridal picturesque to dissolve or disappear before your very eyes as wreckage. You must salvage the wreckage, remember the covenant has been entered into faithfulness is required and demand, no falseness and betrayal by either party. It is a matter of facing death other than wreckage, should be your identity. Do not take the cowardice robe.

All of us have had disappointing experiences of one kind or another, for all of us do have our spots and wrinkles but are we to be ruined by them as waves at sea? We do taste of devastating extremes which we possibly ignored and no doubt, is the cause of wreckage.

Filled with powerful supercharge assurances quite blindly, cause under harassing circumstances become unfriendly which results in a wreckage. However, it implies that I am confident that the store house of blessings is always opened to salvage the wreckage. Mr. Right, there is plenty of fishes left in the sea. Compromise, is a very important vehicle to good relationships.

In a wreckage, lots of debris keep drifting around which will happen to be in the way as obstacles and add to the already distress and perhaps confusion on hand. Old people say" when life gives you lemon make lemonade" in short, when there is a tragedy of sunken-ship, then turn it into a triumph by salvaging the wreckage. Bring it to a speedy end.

In another section of this book, you were urged to avoid a separation and evade a divorce. However, at this point based on, should you suffer at the hand of a separation or wreckage, you must make efforts to have this resolved in a unification of the parties in an amicable manner.

To every reader these information and guides go beyond the mind's gate as an individual and you are asked to represent this work and at the same time, to help others to understand it and develop it in his or her life style.

Marriage does not intend to MAR (impair) RI—AGE (not to mar your age) but rather, a new identity for husband and wife and not separation, divorce or shipwreck, if so, this will mean a newer identity. Remember, before marriage, you were for yourself but after marriage you belong to another. Hence, in wreckage, you are no longer together in unity in what so ever you do but instead you have gone back to the past and let me remind you that no one could live in the past or future but only in the present.

Wreckage, or no wreckage, you must be careful for there are many materials out there also numberless attractions to tempt you to numerous pit-falls. Do not permit wreckage to drive you into a solitary wilderness of grief. You are husband and wife and you provide the grains for your vineyards. All are therefore yours, don't let it go. You are forever, the bridegroom. However, in wreckage, who will do the grooming? Are these to be left for someone else to do? The vicious circle of wreckage is vanity.

Please, bear in mind, that my presentation is LOVE, which is head of this family. It is not factory nor a manufacturer, but a natural inborn togetherness as a living corporate entity and not a mere cooperation. As you see it, it must not be just an ordinary organization but as a genuine active organism.

It is love that is candidly, sincerely and constructively founded, that will only then be truly lasting with all its attributes and splendor, coupled with satisfaction. No room is there left for entertain a wreckage. Our undivided and active Love and indulgences must not be a hinderous tradition, which binds us to be counterproductive with none authoritative proof which is the result of a wreckage, but basically, my opinion is when it is sincerely founded. Don't you believe that LOVE is a sound architecture and best solution in this dire time of need? Will you not acknowledge and use this prescription? For the ingredients are proportionate and is a balanced diet necessary for perfect health. You have it, where will you go in search for what you already have but are not doubt just asleep.

Wreckage is somewhat scaring and is on the negative side, while love is the life force blossomed and blooms with the beauty and nectar of health. But wreckage is a cancer when allowed to develop, cure it and you actually defend your reputation against malicious gossip and dark alleys. True wealth begins with Love and kindness ripple forth to take in abundantly vast pool of shared love voluntary with simplicity is a manner of living what is outwardly more visible and simple, but inwardly, more satisfying and rewardingly rich. It is not about living in isolation and poverty but being in a balance.

A house that you may fill with overpriced furniture—a large television set and costly utensils etc. that is larger than your resource of income, will contribute to pollution and wreckage. It must not be forced on you and there should be abuse to result in a breach. If there is no cheese, then there is no bread. Swallow the words you hear and be successful. However, a stressful career could be an effort to be more meaningful, although it may be very dull, be on the lookout for these could be the end of your heart and love will always meet you and no ruin will take its place.

You can suppress or cure wreckage with patience, understanding, love, tolerance, acceptance, kindness, courtesy, smiles, joy, happiness, comfort and peace of mind. Each choice we make can change our lives. It influences the people we love, the path we take and the way we go about it. What is important in life does not know the meaning of something, but in effect on you that counts. There will be times when you want to rage, cry or scream at what life hands you; some situations ruin the best of your life.

You, as people whether in a jungle or in a city would share the same emotions such as love and hate, joy and sorrow, kindness and self-interest, a desire for personal freedom and for power over others. These ingredients are no respecter of person and embrace all class of people, both the young and the old.

Surely, I have warned you, give examples and provide enough for your safe journey.

Chapter 22

Scenes of Post Marriage

Since I have covered the point where the two parties have come together, this work should have been closed but, it would be an abrupt end and quite a few important points and guides would still wanting as a result, I have to go to the Post Marriage Era, because what is to be brought out in this section could not have been rightly treated elsewhere.

As I am writing on the opening subject, it is preferable therefore; that I could confine myself to it and not to treat such other related matters fully as sexual and styles or methods, disease and ailments of both men and women. Female systems of pregnancy, care of the young child, care of the mother etc., these you will find in the books on the shelves and by consulting a doctor.

I do not want to look into general problems, such as a lazy husband or wife, drunkard-ness, adultery, third party affairs, go between, which promotes disputes and unhappiness, woman who wants to be the ruler and boss and very often takes the husband's place, which are all side effects upon the patient.

My desire is to bring you to the knowledge of the hidden or secret matters which are not normally found in a book on this work but rather is to be gained though experience, which is no doubt base on trials and errors, and surely is the norm in all fields in everyday life.

After marriage, the first sexual intercourse, will take place at these times, the first penetration into the maiden vagina of the young girl will bring forth pain, due to the expansion of a narrow passage and bleeding slightly because of the punctured hymen. This minor problem must not be taken too seriously because the slight burning pain and bleeding will be of in a short duration and even the pleasure may supercede those introductory feelings, which will happen only on the first occasion.

Child bearing may follow any time and when it does, it could be had at your choice, this means that you could have a child when you desire and further, the gender that is, whether, a son or a daughter. Of course, doctors will disagree, choosing the type of a child gender wise. Your desire is based on certain natural line of actions and manipulations and techniques, upon the partner. Although, bearing in mind that you are not GOD and you cannot perform a miracle. However, within God's natural law, should you know how to apply it, then you could influence the course and outcome of your desire and efforts.

Hence, Because of this arousing, the male sperm which could move or swim by itself, by a whip like lashing of the tail, will reach first to the matured female egg, release by the two ovaries as it travels through the fallopian tube which opens into the uterus or womb. Fertilizations take place in the fallopian tube by the male sperm, which reaches the egg before the round germ of the female.

After this, germination it cannot be implanted in the fallopian tubes. If it does, it will cause a serious situation and emergency surgery has to be done to avoid death. By means of the little hair-like organs, called cilia in the fallopian tube waving back and forward, carries the ripen eggs or ovum which may have been penetrated by a visible or live sperm into the womb and thus, pregnancy occurs.

By now, you will have understand that a female germ or even a girl child under normal conditions, by the passionate foreplay, the male sperm will be awaken and thus propel itself at a faster rate. One of the best and quickest ways to put her into that high passion is to fondle with the clitoris but this must be done very lightly, so as to avoid tenderness or blisters to the vagina perhaps with her consent.

Should you wish to have a son? Then, it will depend heavily on your foreplay, such as kissing, caressing, fondling or sucking her nipples, play with her breast and do such other decent acts attached to sexual foreplay which will drive her into a high heat and crazy desire for intercourse on her part, on her face, in her eyes, looseness in her entire body and much natural lubrication of her vagina can be observed, if you are keen. At this point of time you must have intercourse with her, make sure that you control yourself and do not go into her before she reaches the above sensations and climax and desired pitch, because by then, you will also reach that high pitch that is necessary by both parties before sexual intercourse could be had.

If, she does conceive, it will be a son. If, on the other hand you are highly heated and she is cool or loop-warm, then she is not quite mindful for intercourse and you go into her at that stage, when she should conceive, it will be a daughter. The girl child shows that only the man was in the mature sexual passion, while a son born will indicate that both the female and male were in a high sexual passion at the time of sexual intercourse.

The fore-play, stimulate the lazy sleepy male sperm and it will become very active than the female germ, the female reproductive system, among other organs, consists chiefly of a pair of ovaries, a pair of fallopian tubes, the uterus or womb, the vagina, external genitals, the hymen and some other glands. The release of mature eggs or ovum, from the ovaries usually occurs at about the mid-point of the menstrual cycle on a monthly basis, although, there could be variations of dates. This exercise is called ovulation.

The external genitals of the female is known as the vulva and it includes the labia or lips and covers the clitoris, which is at the far top forward fold of it. This clitoris or organ is the homologue. This is a similar structure to the male penis because it consists of erectile tissues, which responds like the penis to sexual stimulation by becoming engorged with blood and is very sensitive to the touch. It could be easily aroused to a very passionate desire for sexual intercourse. All sexual stimulation or acts of masturbation or self-relief could be achieved by playing with it.

A little about the hymen or maiden head, it is a thin vale which partly closes the vagina and at all means intercourse for this first time bound to puncture it before entering into the female sexual passage.

When this happens sexually, she is no more a virgin, but on the other hand, if it is loss without sexual intercourse, she is still a virgin. Unfortunately, her husband may not accept her as such. However, whether so, or not in the sight of God, she is a virgin.

Sperm or spermatozoa, is the fully developed male sex cell, formed in the testes and if viable or alive, is capable of fertilizing his fertile female egg or ovum and is found in abundance in the semen. It is a spear shape head, a neck and a thread like tail. In short, it is similar to a tadpole except in color.

It appears, that the medical science has not yet traced or discovered how to successfully choose or trace or influence the sex before birth, which have to be done as I am saying, during sexual foreplay and manipulations. According to the medical science, the controlling of the sex of their off springs at conception is somewhat remote, if not impossible.

The female cell contains two determines (chromosomes) for sex, which the body of the male has one determine and when the egg cell is produced from the female ovary, it contains one of these determines. The male sperm cells are made of half, having one sex determine and of the other have none. So, when the sperm with one sex chromosomes meets an egg cell which always contains one determine the fertilized egg cell which will have two and is therefore, female germination and on the other hand if the sperm cell has no sex chromosome, which is also produced by the male and a male child will be expected. It will be recalled that the male produced both the male and female germs.

The female always a female determine, when the female germ produced in the womb, and then the birth will be a female. When the male sperm which propels with its tail, should reach the fertile egg first, then a male sperm and cause the race of winning for survival, because only the one that reaches first will germinate and survive, because only the one survive, therefore, thereafter all the rest will die within seventy two hours and is passed out through the menstrual fluid.

In my opinion, a female child is always easier to rear and she grows at a faster rate with less overall problems. A male is easier to be aborted from the womb and more difficult to care for and succumb to infections more quickly.

CHAPTER 23

Bring out your beauty with the natural and simple beauty hints.

Every woman in particular no matter if ugly, wants to be recognized and told at least by someone that she is beautiful and because of this, she does not depend or rely wholly on her natural beauty, but revert to artificial make ups, cosmetics, perfume, hair-do, dress etc. all in the interest to attract or cause a curious eye of the opposite sex to admire and appreciate her as a love partner. Even a fancy style of walking may be adopted to command or motivate some male who is out there and may also be starving for love.

Is it possible for you to identify a young woman, who is not guilty of what is written here? Should you see two girlfriends walking together on an outing, and it happened that a boy passes by and show some interest in one of them and the other friend, who is not admired one should go and have a chat with that boy, later she rejoins her waiting friend, what do you expect will flow from the admired girl? Well, it will be lots of questions to the conversing friend. All aimed to get from her as to how the boy feels about her, what he thinks of her, does he love or appreciate her and what he said about her etc. etc.

While my expressions and presentations may not be impressive as an educationalist, nevertheless, I have presented the facts quite clear to you as they come to mind. "Beauty is like a caged bird, which one day, will take to its wings and fly away". What is then left for you to boast about? This saying is true as it goes, even to all of us as a whole for both man and woman because all of us are going to fade away as the beautiful flowers fall to the ground. Although we are aware of the above, they will continue to the end, they are old as the world itself, and never-the less, at every new love that springs up, it becomes refreshing as the morning dew on your flower garden. Each is exciting and an admiration of its own.

Here are some dos and don'ts that will help you keep in good health and beauty.

(1) Do you suffer with oily skin or face? Then, do not eat much animal fat nor use much sugar, fried foods, soft drinks, candy and processed foods. Concentrate on fresh fruits and vegetables and their juices, fresh greens and fish, poultry and brewer's yeast. You should rinse your face with cider vinegar and fresh cool water. You can also clean your face with a slice of potato or fresh tomatoes. Leave on the face for about thirty minutes before washing off.

(2) If soap is a danger or that you are allergic to it, when rinsing your face, after using face make ups, or if it is oily, then you could mix a teaspoon of skim milk powder in some like warm water to a milky consistency and apply gently, rubbing with a ball of cotton wool to the affected parts.

(3) For red capillaries, commonly called red veins on the face, which is a sign of vitamin deficiencies, commonly it could be remedied by vitamin c. Rutin, which are parts of the bio-flavoroid family and B-complex.

(4) For sallow or discolored skin (face) blend a tablespoon of yogurt with a teaspoon of yeast, rub in on face and leave for forty minutes then rinse, first with like warm water, followed by cool water, then dry with a sturdy towel.

(5) An excellent toner is water melon or muskmelon for dry winter skin commonly called or known as winter flakes with a constant shedding tendency. The best thing in this case is to keep away for musing processed and starchy foods and turn to fresh fruits and vegetables with unsaturated oil daily along with pure fish or cod-liver oil or olive oil placed on

the face, massage the face with a rich make up of egg, oil and lemon juice as often as possible continue to use until the skin becomes natural again.

(6) You are aware that moisturizer of vegetables, seed or nut oil, olive and fish oil will keep the skin soft, premature skin and facial wrinkles which is no doubt caused by sun bathing, (over exposure to ultra violet rays) are a set back to the female beauty. First step is to desist from these types of im-moderate exposures for they cause dry skin and instead to use in your diet each day two to three table spoons of vegetable oil, which will work wonders for raspy, dry skin and dry hair. A vitamin E supplement will contribute a far way in improving the situation.

(7) Treatment for a rough skin: Apply powered almond or corn starches to your wet face at bed time and gently rub in until it foams, thereafter you could rinse off with like warm water followed with cold water.

(8) Acne and whitehead: This could be embarrassing and where antiseptic lotion, medicated cream and other face make up or remedies have failed. You could turn to the application of B2 vitamin (riboflavin) food intake, which will help. This is found in wheat germs, liver and yeast in a proper proportion and balance.

(9) Another embarrassment to you, is if someone is to grumble or remark to you that you have fouled or bad breath, even body odor and I think this may very well interfere with a happy home life because you cannot curdle and kiss freely, as you are aware, this kind of manipulation is essential in all love affairs and its absence, is truly dangerous and do not harbor well for the couple. This could briefly be divided into three categories:-

(1) Decayed tooth and this could be extracted.
(2) Thickly coated tongue, the sediment of which should be scraped out every morning.
(3) Internally bad breath from the stomach also inclusive of the body odors.

Here is a natural way to help combat this dreadful and offensive smell quickly, besides your usual bath and external perfumes, you are to take to internal treatment with chlorophyll tablets or the young green tops or sprouts of plants, or alfalfa, along with thymol which is extracted from garden plants or the mint family and mouth refreshing flavors and raw sugar.

CHAPTER 24

Dispute guidelines

In the chapters, "The Red Road and Broken Home", I treated and put up suggestions on how to save the marriage and avoid separation, while in this chapter "Disputes Guidelines"—are given to a mediator and at the same time, the separated couple could take full use and advantage of the outlined suggestions, thereby avoiding a third party mediating in a family dispute or an actual separation between a man and a wife. In fact, you do not in true sense amend the difference of these parties nor do you have the solutions. You only have suggestions and maybe with healthy guidelines, which of course, are useful and would help the willing parties to resolve their differences and so make amends.

The remedy then, rest between the two affected persons and once they could see this prescription and make use of it coupled with the determination for an amicable settlement, which are solely theirs, then the seemingly difficulties and impossibilities would be removed by this detergent and once again, they will be together as husband and wife under one roof on one bed, eating from one preparation, leading normal, loving and happy life. Where bygones, are bygones. As a matter of fact, if true love exist, although there are occasional interruption by not seeing each other, when it happens there will be an immediate stimulus for a reunion.

Here is a typical example of how to approach and go about the matter as a go between person. First, no mediator whether man or woman are to set in any manner, whatsoever as to fix his or herself as a lover. You are not to make love or courting any of the parties during your intervention as a peace maker. It is important to meet and have discussions with each person separately, maybe, including any of each side relative at this early stage. By this it is meant, not to include a relative from the man's side, when discussing the problem with the woman. Only the woman's relative could be present and such a person is to be a confidential one and to have the approval from the affected wife as to be present through the proceedings. This similar approach is to be done on the husband's side. Try at all times to be a very small group, if it should be necessary for additional family member to be present. Please do not inter-mix the relative at this early stage.

Maybe, it may even be better to exclude a family or relative of either the husband or the wife because of privacy. Why? Because at some point in time at any given moment that family member been privilege with the most private information can create an embarrassment in the event of a dispute or misunderstanding as the "big gossip" in the same small knitted society they resides. This may or may not happen but as a precaution you are to choose well who should be present listening to your

The difference between male and female as humans are that the male is the breadwinner and the wife is the next builder. A wife always feels that the other woman or wife is better off in life than she is and with this plaguing consciousness she will ruin herself. Every man, woman and child seek happiness, joy, fulfillment in life. We must look through the smoke to see where the fire is and try to understand what caused it and quickly put it out with water and not fuel.

Here are some useful hints and questions to ask, not necessary in this sequence, both the wife and husband separately. Not in the presence of each other, or to the knowledge of each other at this early stage and no arrangement should be made for them to be face to face at the beginning. Also, you should not disclose the answers you get from one party to the other party until you are finally through with them both and when you would have bought them together.

Having asked the wife questions, you will have to go to the husband and ask him the very questions to get his response and you will find that both parties do honestly want to re-unite. Having all the facts from both sides, you are now ready to close the wide gap by bringing both parties together face to face. You are to do all, or most of the talking which would be brief and to the point,

You should not permit a constant repetition or rehearsal of the problems from the couples (say, the wife or the husband), constant reflection on what caused the aggrieved problems would only aggravate the already sore heart. It is a time when the cause should be quickly forgotten and set aside, for those causes had now become history, being in the past. Let it be the mirror of self-examination, for corrections rather than to be a quagmire to stall the whole process.

Very often, the woman who from anger could hardly control her emotions will want to keep speaking and repeating and give vent to her feelings about the matter that caused the quarrel, followed by the separation or annoyance. Nevertheless, you are to put a halt to that behavior, never entertain the grievous and un-called for provocation. Although, it could be regarded as war, it is somewhat different in the peace mission from that between two nations fighting for power and to bring their fellow-men under subjection unlike that this is a LOVE BATTLE and a venture to reunite the two parties without suspicion distrust, fear or favor and ill-will. Rehearsal, in a drama is good but in this case, it is a deadly poison, which will kill the hope of a settlement or at least, make the exercise more difficult. Without touching any controversial questions because both sides had already agreed to set the problems aside. Remind them in the areas where both parties had one common ground of agreement while you were narrowing the gulf off separation with your firm desire to reunite in a loving home that both of them had built and so you can personally say "this is the house that Jack built".

The wife needs to be reminded, that the marriage ring made of pure gold is placed on her finger is a custom by the Egyptians down to our present day as a "token" meaning that he has entrusted her with all his properties, and the authority to use his name unrestricted in the marriage ceremony likewise, follow the custom and the man places the ring when he reaches the point and says "with all my worldly good I thee endow". It is a scared moment when two people who are strangers to each other, are drawn together by an irresistible attraction for life, would you not say, jack live in this house that Jack built?

The woman needs to be reminded, that the marriage ring shows that the man has a claim on her and because the house had been broken down, it must be reconstructed and because it is an emergency, you have to use suitable and available material to rebuild it, less you have no shelter to rest your weary self, and no pillow to rest your aching head, for sweet dreams and a peaceful sleep.

Here are some questions to guide you in your venture of rebuilding or patching up or remolding your broken marriage. Honestly answer yes or no.

(1)   Do you think you are permanently separated?

(2)   Is this the end of the road for you?

(3)   Do you wish, for your marriage to be broken up or destroyed?

(4)   How do you feel without your mate?

(5)   Are you lonely and do you miss your mate?

(6)   Do you long to see your husband and for him to be back in your life?

(7)   Don't you believe you would live to regret separation?

(8)   Do you truly want back your husband?

(9)   Do you want for both of you to live together again?

(10) Should you separate from this husband, are you going to take another?

(11) Do you think you can live and get along without a husband?

(12) Don't you think worst advantage could befall you as a single person?

(13) Don't you think you may be tempted to live an unsettled life?

(14) As a single parent, you alone would have to provide for the children and yourself. Do you think you can manage with all that?

(15) Do you foresee, through separation that you may be lucky to have better second husband? Some persons are lucky.

(16) Do you think the changes of separation are worth to venture?

(17) Don't you believe separation is a mistaken gamble?

(18) Do you think it is better to leave what you have and to go in search for what you do not know and assume to be good or better?

(19) Is not the bird in the hand is worth two in the bush?

(20) Do not your own half, better than the whole that belongs to someone else?

(21) Do you acknowledge your mistake?

(22) Are you conscious of your areas of wrong doing?

(23) Are you prepared to correct those wrongs?

(24) Do you truly promise to set them aside and never let them shoot up again—come hell fire?

(25) Do you truly promise to keep your promises?

(26) Do you promise that you will never allow anything harmful to go between you and your husband again?

(27) Do you prepare to accept your husband if he is prepares and agrees to return?

(28) Are you prepared to make personal sacrifices so that your marriage could last in happiness, will you part until death?

(29) Do you know the faults of your husband?

(30) Are you prepared to overlook his faults?

(31) Would you agree to accept him to set those faults aside before you would agree to his return?

(32) Do you want him to set those faults aside before you would agree to his return?

(33) What are his most disturbing faults?

(34) What things aggravate you and get you annoyed most?

(35) What things are pleasant to you?

(36) If he corrects only some of his faults would you still try to understand and to abide and to live along together?

(37) Do you promise not to repeat those faults time and again?

(38) That separation must not be the foremost thought in the mind in the future?

(39) That you will never leave the matrimonial home again?

(40) That you will never again let the sun set on your wrath?

(41) That immediately, you must replace all wraths with love.

(42) That there must be no more nagging and quarrelling.

(43) That no gossiping and third party are to be entertained.

(44) No evil allegations are to be indulged in.

(45) What suggestions do you have that could cause yourself and husband to reconcile matter and permanently forget and forgive each other and cause both of you to re-unite as husband and wife?

(46) Suppose your husband never correct his faults but he still wants you, are you still prepared to reunite with him? Even to his faults or yours would you demand that all his faults be first corrected?

(47) That you must not reunite with him or her because of someone else, say children or parents because there will still be future problems?

(48) Do you believe that there is a solution to your home problems?

(49) Do you believe that neither of you should rush outside of the home and jump to conclusions and hope to find agreeable and suitable fulfillment in life?

(50) Don't you think that you will be respected better with one husband or wife in your life except in the case of a second husband or wife though death?

(51) Should your husband or wife ignore you, what should be your action for the future life?

(52) Don't you think the first separation would have an adverse effect on your second marriage?

(53) Don't you think your second husband or wife, shortly after this marriage may throw unbearable remarks about your first marriage?

(54) Do you see that although you are together, you are still far apart?

(55) Do you know, some husbands and wives do not communicate with each other for months and also do not sleep together nor dwell together etc. Although, they are still under the same roof and should there be a visitor

in the home and no one would detect the problems are existing. Are you guilty of this behavior?

(56) For every problem, there is a reason and for every such cause there is a solution. Yet, no one understands what the real solution is, for it may not always work out the way you think or want it to be. Yet, the outcomes will have to be accepted as the solution.

(57) Many husbands or wives are not truly fit to be husbands or wives. However, unfortunately it is human to go to extreme only to realize this wrong when the damages are already done.

(58) Do you know that even the best marriages are the product of pulling and dragging at times?

(59) So you know that it takes a lot of sacrifices and input by both parties to repair the damages?

(60) Are you going to say that my marriage is far better or worse and say as a young man replies "yes but she is worse than I took her for"?

(61) Do you see and understand that marriages should be every body's business because its effects are of a wide range. At a divorce, the outcome of a broken marriage, several persons are sad, every time a house is destroyed, the nation suffer, the child quakes in fear because of a broken home even god's business, because he created male and female, so that none will be lonely?

(62) A ruin marriage is not always caused by unfaithfulness or desertion but it could be a slow accumulation of misunderstandings, petty criticism and irritations that expand in to dissatisfaction which reach explosion point, where neither could hear it any longer thereby the inevitable alternative is to seek redress in separation.

(63) Marriage is a sacred circle and a circle has neither beginning nor an ending and when that circle is broken, it is indeed hard to repair.

(64) Do you know what ever gets on your mind gets you? Because it is you who placed it there, likewise, whatsoever captures your imagination, embraces you until you repel then, from you inner self, why not do so quickly?

(65) Are you aware, that every time you think right, you strengthen the hope for better and anytime you decide wrongly, you weaken your chance to succeed?

(66) Do you know, that very often in an unstable home disputes are not set aside, the causes are ignored and the attacker turns to personal abuse and attack, which drives severe blows and penetrates very deep then the tragedy answers loud and clear with other parties going in different directions, for unity is then absent?

(67) When your husband or wife is speaking to you, are you present, do you hear what was said or are you running an errand in the mind? Pretense playing games and wearing mask will not do. Honesty at the point is exceptionally important, if an amicable settlement is to be reached at the conference table.

(68) Do you want a physical war in the battlefield where lives are destroyed?

(69) Are you aware that great damages are done at the battlefield but at the conference table is where the battle is amended?

(70) No one party is always right or wrong nor is a hundred percent right or wrong.

(71) Do you wish me to arbitrate in this your problem and are you prepared to accept and go by my findings?

(72) As a mediator, you must be meticulous person because any sign of weakness would arouse abuse upon yourself and lost confidence in you to further mediate.

(73) If you do not have confidence in me then it will be a waste of time for me to intervene.

(74) Do you agree, if you continue take on your home worries, you would be destroying your own self and this could reach a far way with disturbing effects?

(75) Which method is disgraceful, to separate or to reunite in the home?

(76) Do you imagine or even claim that your partner loves an outsider than for you?

(77) Do you suspect and distrust your spouse of having an affairs or cheat on you? Do you believe that all the problems

could have been avoided, for the want of a little more interest, care and patience?

(78) Have you ever look into the areas of each other's likes and dislikes and use these findings to the best advantage of getting better?

(79) Are you guilty of joining with outsiders to say evil of your spouse?

(80) Don't you think that if you accept your spouse good qualities then you will also have to tolerate the bad ones?

(81) Did you ever find out from your spouse, what are your bad qualities with a view to correct them?

(82) Do you speak soft, mild with a smile and a sign of love and kindness and courteous-ness, or driving fear with every word from your mouth?

(83) What are the changes for the worst did you spouse made between your marriages to the time of separating?

(84) Did you from time to time ever draw to your spouse attention in a lively, cool atmosphere of the contrary behavior inclusive of its likely behavior in your life style?

(85) Was the war-path, the only way for you?

(86) Are you going to look to others and adopt their pattern or implement their behavior in your life style?

(87) Don't you believe that your own working out of a solution could bring a more genuine and peaceful settlement of peace and joy?

(88) Are you inclined to be enticed by an intruder, who may be painting a rosy picture to you and shower you with gold, moon and the stars and a heaven of perceptual bliss, all for his or her own selfish gain and at this time may even paint your spouse with tar?

(89) Don't you think, you should be more careful, cautious and access well, all matters before and that this may be too early a stage in your broken home to take a rash conclusion against your spouse?

(90) Did you ever consider, that similarly, how your spouse leave you for another, in like manner that spouse could

leave another person for another person and goes down the line as a rolling stone?

(91) Are you a person who worries over spilt milk?

(92) Do you ever consider that you should first humble yourself and make the move towards reconciliation?

(93) Do you think that you should go against the tide or to kick against the prick?

(94) From all these many questions, don't work out agreeable and well-balanced solutions, which will put an end permanently to the present and future problems?

(95) Did you know that in match marriage, you did not do the loving of your spouse but someone else did the loving and you the marriage?

(96) Do you know that in match marriage you marry not to please yourself but, someone else?

(97) Do you know, in match marriage, true love and sincere love do develop later on in life?

(98) Did you marry for love or revenge?

(99) Do you agree, that neither of you understand or know your true love for each other, so your misunderstanding is due to petty love quarrels?

(100) Remember, love is not based on the enslaving or dictating or imprisonment of the husband, wife or child.

Be on the alert, if a YES is the answer given, when there should be a NO and if NO answer is given to these questions where a YES should be, then it is definite that a peace is not truly desired and is heading for the rock bottom and that a settlement if still pursued, would entail difficulties to have amends.

CHAPTER 25

An answer LOST—How to FIND Back Your PATH

The short account of the foundation and progress of this subject must be studied from interest rather than compulsion. My own experiences impel me to emphasize the discretion, which goes beyond the confine and individualism. Wealth and power of any kind would never the less begin by adventure across the sea and by so doing, ambitious ones will find an outlet. There will be no dull seclusion as with the home staying craftsman. Explorers (for that is what you are) you cannot limit your energies of romance, until the fusion of both passionate love explodes.

You are to be nervous, suffer from inferiority complex and become sexually impotent from fear. Stop dreaming dreams and promptly sought to realize them by setting sail across the unknown successful and in triumph of succulent love. Throughout the centuries, curiosity aroused by conjecturers (guesswork) that the subject is frequently a source of mystification to those un-versed in ways of good love and good lovemaking.

To most modern mind, it appears to be meaningless and is somewhat felt an exaggerated importance, rather than truly important and that is automatic and attached to trifles. Yet, it is the most interesting art manipulation in the evaluation of the development towards mastering of good love making from the rough untrained ways or methods of premature man, as against the disciplined and politeness, which are always necessary in love making. "manners maketh man" and also etiquette, goodness with gentleness and simplicity are workable charms worthy of their merits as golden rules.

In the different mediums of communication you will find broken lovers, who give vent to their good or their evil haunts and love and nightmares, which could be sensitivity avoided or at least minimized. The good ones are happy people and that is how it is to be but again, those on the bad side of the love world, are indeed touching, and heart breaking and sad. Let us therefore, reflect a little on their plight, which destroys many lives that succumb to it.

I said before, that the two lovers involved, are the only persons that have the solution in themselves and could make things work out favorable and avoid a break up in their love affairs. There are several cases where a man loves two or more girls. Of course, it is a mistake and this is confusion because he does not want to lose any of them. It is very difficult for him to decide which one to marry. Well, only you have the answers. A diligent and careful examination of all the girls in question along with the application of my advice mentioned elsewhere in this book, will help to solve that problem very quickly and amicable.

My hints to you, is that with that careful search you will discover that you love one of them more than the rest and from there you take the other step by checking the chapter "How to choose a partner" or at least if all things go well and coincide with the advice given, then you should settle for that one to be your love partner or at least from there. You can analyze each one's character and there after you can take your pick and even if the dice should fall on the one you do not love, I would suggest that you change your heart towards her and go for that love and from thereon, you are to develop yours and her love to grow the way you want it to be.

Many girls also fall in the same love dilemma and are also selfish and do want both lovers, not realizing in what dangerous waters they fish in. Surely, you cannot marry both lovers. Follow the above guide lines given for men and stable yourself early before it is too late and un-heal-able damages are being done. It is observed that this state of affairs very often come about, because the lineup of suitors—love will comprise of many examples maybe one that is poor financially, one that is maybe richer than them, all in the things that are essential for a loving and peaceful home.

The rich person will rely heavily on his money to spend lavishly on you and actually purchase you without you knowing it. The handsome one will manipulate on his beauty and here you may go all out for him. You have to be very careful an observant because it could very well be false love. You will find that the ugly one will be more kind and loving because sincerity and loyalty are what they have to decide on taking your pick and do not be unevenly yoked.

There are exceptions. I am not saying that the rich or handsome persons do not make good lovers to a poor girl who is often led away by money, which is mistaken for love. When you are poor and less beautiful than they are, very often they rebuke you and they are full of competition, which ends with numberless and untold problems later on. Do your best to get along and save your marriage or intended marriage.

I remember a story when I was a child growing up, where Bear-Anancy rode Bear-Tiger, who was claiming to be the king, he rode him all over town and Bear-Tiger became the laughing stock by the people of that city while Bear-Anancy enjoyed himself on the back of Bear-Tiger. Several rounds were made through the city and that surprised all the viewers. Similarly, you the female, who allow extreme passion to overtake you, it will take you for a jolly mockery ride with a slap in the face of downright shame and molestation to be followed with regrets.

Ladies and men, you are to keep cool and calm and show and give more love to each other, because this will bring about a quick amendment and your desire will be fulfilled by your most wonderful charm. Should you stop accidentally or willfully to look at any person making love, you will be called a "peeping tom" and you will feel ashamed but should you educate yourself by reading these information's found in this book, you will be looked upon as wise man or woman, having fill your empty storehouse with wisdom to be used during a famine, a drought, a storm or a hurricane.

All creation is blessed to go and multiply. It has room well prepared for everyone, no matter who you are, where you are, when or why you cannot tell. Why complain and yell, just answers the bell and you shall be in heaven do not make it a hell.

The newspapers column, according to what the complaints say rightly gets a physiological reply as against this book and chapter which provide the rightful answers from experience and they will cure the lover in distress and perplexity. For instance:

(1) Some females take to heart, after sexual intercourse that they may be pregnant or that they may have contacted a social disease. This may be true or untrue, you are to promptly see your doctor, who will examine you and give you advice or treatment. This thing can cause a fear of fulfilling future sexual desires. The best thing to do in such case is to think well before you attempt to have intercourse or that you should have no intimate contacts or if you cannot control yourself or your desires, then you should use a protection or a condom.

(2) You can conceive, if you have intercourse several times or once as a matter of fact, if you have had intercourse several times, it is during one of those times several contacts, you will get pregnant, if you and your mate is fertile and this could also happen although you did not have any orgasm (break) should you have intercourse during the unsafe or conception periods, the best thing to do is to avoid or take the precautions given in this work.

(3) Many men lovers, are bullies, they demand sexual intercourse and a must and first thing while that should be the last thing to be rightly done and not until after your marriage and not during courtship. The premarital, sexual intercourse, which is the trend nowadays with youths is either consented to or more often forced upon you and or when the girl is fearful of losing her lover she goes out of her way to hold him and so give him a premarital intercourse.

(4) Secret lovers: it is a mistake, when you do not want your parents or guardians to know that you are having a boyfriend or that you are getting a baby. It is something that should never happen in the first place. However, it had and it will also continue to be so. You are to avoid it by informing your parents or guardians early seek their

advice and that should they not appreciate the love affairs of your choice then it could be ended before it develop too strong. The parent's duties are to watch over their children but although they do wish and want the best for them, they could be too strict at times and they must understand that each person have their own life path to mold and live. So they are to limit themselves to offer advice and if that is ignored by the child, then they are not to interfere further.

(5)   If you are pregnant, after one of the secret affairs, you should not have an abortion, as long as you are in good health. If you are now afraid that your parents will discipline you and put you out of their protection. What are you going to do? If this happens, plus the child's father do not want to own the expected child and he will not maintain you nor the child—are all the things you should have pondered over from the beginning and should not have been carried away by the flattering words and empty promises coupled with the passion to satisfy your sexual needs and or desires. All of which based only on deceptive love clothe under a false coat.

(6)   Suppose you were sexually abused or interfered with, by your father or an uncle or a brother, or someone other than a relative or even a stranger by consent, just because you were inexperienced or even if you were being raped. It is a wrong done to you which cannot be undone so you will have to abide with it on your conscience as a result; you are to act as if nothing had happened to you. But you should go right ahead to enjoy the rest of what life has to offer.

(7)   If you are under their control or under duress—illegal compulsion, then do your best at the slightest available opportunity and escape from them immediately, particularly after reading what is said herein. The only way you will remain, is if you like the sport. Should you escape you should expose what happened to you either to other relatives or to the police.

(8)   Love is master of both young and old and you young girls have to be on guard, particularly that you are experience and look for men who are honest and who you do need as against those that are dishonest, covetous, deceitful, running and shrewd.

(9)   Me who truly love and desire you for a life partner are going to set in a sincere manner. However, there are others who simply get carried away with your beauty and would only want to get at you. They will be more flattering in their approach. Very often, you had either seen or heard of the many boys who, simply after waging a successful verbal battle and succeed in getting sexual intercourse with you, suddenly, becomes scarce and eventually walk out and leave you, mostly because he afterwards goes around with someone else and when you detect and question him. He will never admit that he is in love with someone else, because he is covetous; he wants you and the other person at the same time. However, sooner or later, he will leave you for the other.

(10) Men, you also will have to do some selection, because out there is also women, who do not really love you, but go all out to get whatever you have to offer. These females luckily, are few and please note that reference is being made about women who are experienced persons and not to girls whose interest is mostly to get fixed to a lover.

(11) Girls are those young females who had no sexual intercourse and you will find that their love affairs would be more sincere with you, but women are those who had sexual relationship and would practice the clever art to take what they can get.

(12) Do you love two persons at the same time? With promises of marriage and do you want to marry both? Are you confused as to which one should marry? Well, the answer is: do not be covetous, do not be long hearted and want everything for yourself. You fully well know that only one person you could sincerely love and legally married. Dismiss the thought that you will marry one and go friendly with the

other. You could only have one. Do not cheat or later you will suffer and the price will be costly.

(13) As you traverse, this short life span on earth, you will see and maybe get to know a lot of things up and down, good and bad maybe, about yourself and maybe, about others. My advice to you, is beware, see and do as if you did not see. In short apply the old saying "Mind your own business" and avoid getting involved in other people's affairs.

(14) To fall in secret love with your best friend lover and relative is not to be. Why should you take away your best friend comfort? Why reap what you did not sow? This is stealing, are you so lazy you cannot prepare and plough your own field? About the other relative—nothing is wrong when the intention is good, sincere and to be a life partner no one is to feel hurt over these love affairs.

(15) The story of love happens every day, for some, it is a hell and for others a salvation and paradise. It could be rigid or flexible and stretches as rubber. It is however, their silent or voicerous. This book will help you to separate the solid grains from the wind-grains.

(16) Parents, children are blessed and cherished gifts. They are not a luxury, a commodity nor a convenience. They look to you for love, guidance and protection and not deception. They need someone to be-trusted and you are the fittest person and the responsible one. Fathers, your daughter are not a wife for you. Mothers, your son are not a husband for you. You already have a wife or a husband that is how you are a father and a mother. How can you face up to society? When in your inner guilt, your daughter is having her father's baby and also, mother you are having a son's baby. Father, when you daughter becomes your wife, you are a coward and a greedy monster and mother, the same goes to you because both of you have devour yourself.

(17) Should another new lover come your way and sincerely fall in love with you. Perhaps, it will invoke a fear, which may strike you. Are you afraid, that he or she may have learnt of your former ordeal and if so, you are afraid that he or

she may walk out on you? This living thought may deter or prevent you from entering the world of love again. Further, whether you should tell him or her of the annoying incident? All, of these will stir a heap of confusion because you know not whom to trust. Your stand on this matter should be as follows if he or she knows about the advantageous affairs that overlook you, then you are to say nothing. Let the other person be the first to break the silence, to speak what he or she knows about it is to ask you what he or she wants to know. At this point, you are to admit the truth and go on to explain what and how it really happened. On the other hand, if he does not know anything, then you are to remain quiet. Always remember, let the sleeping dogs lie. Say nothing let it remain a secret. Do not fly too fast, he who does so goes alone. Do not be the first to disclose what was under lock and key and to be like PANDORA to set trouble free. You are to put on a brass or guilty manner, less you will arouse suspicion, even the way you behave would cause the sleeping volcano to erupt.

Hence, there are thousands of questions and disturbing entities that pass through the lovers' mind and because of frustration a solution appears to be distance away.

(1) A younger lover says, she is beautiful and well-mannered but tries to impress men at parties and goes flirting and chatting with other girls.
(2) A male says, "I am quite cute and a lot of girls love me and go after me, what must I do?
(3) One forsakes me but now returns with plans for our unification at a time when someone new is in my life, what is to be done? For I still love him with the full memories of your happy times together.
(4) The elderly said, "I want some romance in my life".

It will be seen that the same questions keep returning in just another form. So, your answers for all can be found in this very book.

To be successful, one must be sincere and determine to win, for all falls under these three categories. Say, you're a girl in love and is courting. There is another one who is engaged and there is another, who is married. Per chance, you the unmarried were raped by your partner, you would like to know what to do or react towards him in such a situation. Before you could really act or raise an alarm over a secret matter of this nature, you must consider:

(1) That you did not die or is being injured although you may or may not have suffered pain by the animalistic behavior of your loved ones.
(2) Did you in the long run enjoy the ordeal of sexual intercourse or were you too afraid to do so?
(3) Whether, above all things you sincerely or truly love him and wants him to still be your life partner, or you wish to reject him, for hereon, girl or woman will remain strong after she would have gotten over the shock of being raped. Of course, your adverse, head strong and stubborn behavior, or this type of unforgiving would be the beginning of the end for both parties to part. Both of you why not compromise.

In the home, at times you may have to sit together, watch TV together, and actually dwell together during the day while at nights—sleeping time, you are strangers because you act strangely, even if you share the same bed. No one allow their bodies to touch one another this is a love game playing with each other desperately, do not want to be the looser deep down in the heart, each wants to curdle just the first move needed.

Further, aggravation is when she or he walks out of the house and go anywhere she wishes without informing you, and should you be present, and inquire where he or she is going will result in an explosion but do you know, that both parties are fed up with their own behavior and down in their heart, they do not want any further mishaps, because they realize that it will steam roll towards disaster with each person looking at each other with distrust and suspicion that each is seeing another lover, although this is just an empty thought of their inward jealousy for each other.

The man should be gently and patient and loving and never to be a rapist although, surprisingly all who had sexual relations will be raped and was raped. Let me be fair with you. By disclosing to you that every married man, no matter how decent he may be, had raped his wife knowingly or unknowingly at some time or the other. I will now explain. If rape means unconsented intercourse, then, every husband did have forced intercourse with his wife, when she had no inclinations and desire. Also, every woman that had sexual intercourse suffered a RAPE by the breach of her hymen.

Women, do have a way of taking revenge and they do take it before they become forgiving. This is based on their emotions and uncontrolled passion and unless they do that, their passion will not cool down. They do get great satisfaction in their actions and thereafter, they have no malice but become loving again.

All marriages started out with high hopes for betterment, do not let yours be a tug-of-a-war, why should you two grown up lovers hurt each other so much and so far, do not permit a thin unseen wall of stubbornness to be the veil between two matured sincere lovers.

Sex rationing, without approval and maliciously, will surely anchor both persons and it must be recalled, that both parties do have a breaking point, when both partners could recognize that each, was wrong to each other and matters were taken too far apart and just drop the bomb of forgiveness with love and open arms, to receive what belongs to you and say "I am sorry, I love you" and that will do the trick and open the way for the cooler step to be taken where the passion will be a different kind.

You do not want to break up or lose your loved one, so look at your love one, with love and not hatred and passion. See in your love one the love and beauties of beauty blossom, just in front your eyes. Why suffer unnecessary pains and anguish instead of the reward of kindness and love? Eat and drink from the fountain, the fruit of your personal labor. A good lover and loving love maker is like a rare and beautiful flower, their memory is everlasting.

What does your parting day be like? Let me here speak of two streams that is death, which is unavoidable and separation for misunderstanding. What of your parting day based on the cruel blow of death or the very cruel blow of separating by broken love?

It is sad with painful grief and is likening to the setting to the sun and the gruesome seizure of a cold winter night with foul smelling, howling breeze and as though you are surrounded and actually engulfed by ghosts. Here, you are oppressed with the deepest sorrow, perplexed with depression and confusion where all the former shinning lights into a dungeon of darkness. Yes, your treasured souvenir has been shattered.

(18) Are we to live with our in-laws? Mother-in-law, father-in-law, sister-in-law, brother-in-law, inclusive of their children or other brothers and sisters, the answer is NO; this should be avoided at all costs. Relatives should not interfere in, matters between a husband and wife, unless it is for a good purpose. Many good homes are broken up and many great problems arise with the unnecessary intervention of in-laws. As long as you are living with in-laws or even too near them, there are going to be problems form one kind to another with one of them, if not this one, it is the other. Love and peace and will never prevail. The best thing to do, if you could afford it, is to act or get your own shelter and possibly some distance away you are to live from them.

(19) What if a husband does not wish to leave his parents or wants the parents to come along and live with him? It is very clear. If this happens, he belongs to one of the two evils, either he is afraid to manage his own affairs or that he does not sincerely love you as much as the parents and possibly, he distrusts you. A man must decide that after marriage, he should be on his own and will have to provide for his family and nothing is wrong about this.

(20) A question was asked about the intended marriage male age group. I treated this marriage matter in the chapter dealing with "choosing a partner" but I will venture into it to give some more guideline appropriate in this section. I wish to suggest, that the man should not be more than about 10 years senior as a marriage partner. Sex, itself could be enjoyable and undertaken at, and with any person of any age group after puberty. It will be recalled,

that I did refer to the declining period of both man and woman. Their change of life and age-group should be within the suggested average of their declination, so that it will be, on the same range with each other. If the man is too old, say double the age of the woman and he is a moderate nature, sexually, then she will cheat on the man because of his age and possibly, his heath will physically prevent him to fulfill his manhood responsibilities while at the same time he would still have the desired sting for sexual intercourse. His erection, will be slow and with no particular stiffness to the satisfaction of the woman. If he does find penetration, he will finish quickly. Thus, leaving the woman in an unsatisfied heat and this could be very sickening to the woman or a long time. If the woman is a cool natured person, then she will be in a better position to go with an elderly man and she will have her pleasure, to her satisfaction with a good foreplay.

When the man and woman is in the same age group, with the female two years his junior, then they are going to have change of life together or at the same time and rate. Their desires will go together. Therefore, there will be no need for the woman to cheat on him and seek other men to satisfy her sexual passion.

(21) Life is enjoyable in love and peace said the girl but things had changed only, when the man started to cheat. Then the trouble begins because she is afraid of disease, split of love and money and sharing of time with the other one, and she getting the most of everything. Her passion prevents her to display her love to her lover. You answer as a solution is elsewhere in this book.

This chapter was specially prepared to give the solution in a general way to the many problems which troubles the lovers, who seek and need advice when they are at the cross roads, full of frustrations and whatever they do seem to mark on the ice.

This book will never stop love problems or is it the end all. However, should you make use of the given advises, you will be able to have the opportunity to start fresh. Overtime you may stumble, do not get loss in bewilderment and stray away from knowing what to do next. Here, you do have a true friend and companion to stand with you all the way.

In this world of today, in every walk of life and in every considerable field man has before him varieties which is the benefit of multiple choices. Therefore, no one can be left out, or there is no room to feel left out. No one is really ugly, regardless of color or shape, all are handsome and beautiful in their own way and someone out there do cares, this is not an instigator to evil and the cause to jump around but rather, a given opportunity to think before you leap.

Since we do not know what is in store for us in the future, whatever is being done is done in good faith, it could be favorable or unfavorable, whatever the outcome, do not blame yourself for it but rather start again. Give the contents of this book a try.

We are in a world of trials and errors, do not remain a fallen soldier and give up all hope in helplessness. Get up and fight again as though nothing had happened. Some of the tension could be erased should you mitigate, if you can make it possible, to a place where your historical background is unknown.

CHAPTER 26

A Woman Must Know:

1. Put a bible or scissors under the baby's pillow while asleep (to ward off evil).
2. Put a spot of sooth on baby's forehead to avoid bad-eye.
3. While out with baby, if he/she urinates, catch some and rub on the navel.
4. When menstruation is one, do not visit boy-baby before nine days.
5. When outing, if baby falls asleep, call his/her name and say "we are going ".
6. After a lone walk, the father must place his big-toe on the baby's navel if it is large and it will return to normal.

A BRIDE MUST KNOW

1. On the day of wedding, bride must not look her face in the mirror.
2. The bride must not see her wedding ring, her bridal costumes, before the wedding day. She should dress by someone else. She must not bathe herself also.
3. When she goes out of the house. She must not look back.
4. The bride must not dress in the matrimonial home on the wedding day.
5. If dogs are given the wedding cake, then marriage will break up.

6. If unmarried, rings will be on the right hand fingers, but if engaged, the ring will be on the ring finger of the left hand, which will be removed and replaced with the wedding ring. This will be normally a plain ring. The engagement ring can thereafter be worn with the wedding ring on the same finger in order—the wedding ring first-inner, followed by the engagement ring-outer.

7. When the wedded couple kneels before the priest, or marriage officer, which person gets up first, will outlive the other. The one that gets up last will die first.

BIRTH OF A CHILD

1. When a person gets a baby at home or out of the hospital and even in the hospital, if it is convenient for the placenta, commonly known as the after-birth, to be taken home and buried. A fire should be lit on the spot for nine days. Should this fire happen to go out, do not blow it with your mouth because if you do, then you will lose all your teeth at an early age.

2. It is said, if you do not want children quickly, the placenta when buried should be turned down-wards and should no more children be needed, then bury the placenta Turning downwards and cover it with common salt, saying at the same time no more children is needed. Thereafter, it is to be covered with the earth.

3. If the ears give a sudden sharp ringing, somebody is talking your name also, this happens when you sneeze without having a cold. Again, you may be hearing some strange news.

CHAPTER 27

Miscellaneous
Psalms, Prayers etc.

Because this book was given the name "Family Guide" I had to choose a variety of topics to meet the taste of the various readers. I assure you that I was not alone but many others assisted me to arrive at this conclusion.

I was sensitive to the fact, that to enter a profession or engage in a trade or occupation, which one does not eminent suited, one will not succeed. Ignorantly or for convenience, necessity or expediency will end in failures. The result of which you will find yourself fighting against others thinking and claiming that others are faulty and you are the best. Do not condemn yourself or others, let this not be a habit but please, investigate before you conclude right or wrong.

As you read through this work, you may have mixed feelings and perhaps want to ridicule me and at the same time praise me by saying that what is written herein is good and true. It is an excellent paper work because everything is well said and arranged in place, but in reality to practice it out there, with the partner is difficult, hard and maybe impossible. I urge you towards good not evil and if you do not condemn yourself and with a determined mind, make use of the suggestions and advice at the appropriate time, you will then see how things work out exactly and directly in your favor—when frustration was hitting hard at the door.

I say again that these advices are practical experiences. They worked once in the past, be it ancient or recent, they will work again for you and they will continue to work again in the future as long as you want to work them. They are anxiously waiting to work for you and to serve you faithfully and to give of their best as they see you in trouble. You did not call them, they were before you and they will help you in trouble and distress and they come to rescue you. All you have to do is accept their help with belief and faith. You have nothing to lose by so doing, but much to gain and your profits may be larger than you expected.

I was very thoughtful in presenting this section, fearful of the hasty conclusion, excepting of a few so called religionist, who may want to deem it as witchcraft or superstition etc. Stand clear for none of these have scope in this book and if by chance you discovered this type of teaching anywhere or in any part of this book, then just ignore it.

BURNING OF INCENSE

Practically, I had the opportunity to study theology when I came across the ancient customs of burning in incense and I wish to pass these information to the reader because these knowledge are kept as a secret for the privilege few and it could be reached further afield, education wise and assist to remove fear which is due more or less to lack of information.

Of course, some may find it interesting while to others it maybe of very little use. However the outcome will be based on the strength of your own faith and your style must be a godly one. Free from crime, willful sin and there should be nothing to trouble your conscience. There must be no doubt, when undertaking these holy rituals, coupled with a pious life and a rational use of the psalms, will with god's grace, you may gain his favor for your own welfare. I now bring to you the daily burning of temple incense with the rituals of the appropriate psalms to be used between eleven to twelve mid night, which is in your best time being quiet with better concentration.

Sunday: for success in your undertakings, pray psalms fifty six in a low prayerful manner, seven times to twelve times over burning incense regularly, for some weeks. Add your own appropriate prayers.

Monday: to receive knowledge and wisdom, fast for twenty four hours, thereafter bathe and pray fully repeat psalms 23, seven times with your own appropriate prayers and pouring out your heart to god. The holy name to use is JAH.

Tuesday: for the protection against enemies, pray over temple incense ten times. Read psalms fifty three, fifty four, fifty five, six times. This is not to harm your enemies but rather to change their behavior towards you.

Wednesday: to gain knowledge and help in court matters use pray fully psalms 134 five times over temple incense.

Thursday: for general love and love between husband and wife procurement, pray fully use over incense, psalms forty five and forty six. Upon a cross wife use psalms 45 ten times.

Friday: for fortune, might and power, read psalm 112 seven times and psalms 137 nine times over temple incense.

Saturday: in sickness, troubles or evil spirit, pray fully use psalms 90 and 91 four times over incense.

The use of incense and candle were used in the beginning of the world as could be found in the bible Exodus 37-29. Check this for yourself for there are many things contained in this book which could be proven from the bible.

I neither wish to lead you astray with the value of the psalms. You are ignorant of their value and to use them to your advantage although you no doubt, read them often. I merely mention them and wish to assist you, in the direction. You can check the bible for yourself at Ephesians 5-19, Colossians 3-16 and James 5: 13-14. Do not attempt to test yourself or God. They must only be used for genuine purposes and not for vengeance, malice, ill-will or victimization. There are many ways to which man could make use of the psalms in order to get its full benefit. Without further delay here are some of the ways you can use the Psalms:

Psalms 1:   Premature Delivery:
             To avoid premature baby delivery and dangerous
             confinement. Write on parchment verses 1, 2, and 3,
             with the Holy name of EL CHAD, coupled with you
             own suitable prayers. Place in a small sack and rest it
             on the naked body.

Psalms 3:   For Pain:
             To pray over olive oil and anoint affected parts, head
             and back, use holy name ADON with your own suitable
             prayers for pain.

Psalms 6:   For the eyes:
             Prayer for three days, seven times each, singing holy
             name JASCHAJAH, with your own prayer along with the
             psalms 13. Holy name is ESSIEL—good for the eyes.

Psalms 7:   Enemies:
             Against enemies, pray using holy name EEL ELIGON
             with your own prayer.

Psalms 8:   Love from all men:
             To gain love and good will for men, pray for three
             days after sun down. Use holy name RECHIMAIL with
             you own prayer.

Psalms 9:   Child's Health
             To restore a male child's health, pray with holy name
             EIEYE AISCHIEE EHEJE and write with new pen on
             parchment and place under patient's neck also use you
             own prayers. It could be used against you enemies.

Psalms 10:   Evil Spirit:
Against evil-spirit, fill new earthen pot with spring water and write the name of the patient.

Psalms 13:   Eye diseases:
For protect from dangers and eye disease. Pray daily, holy name ESSIEL, use own suitable prayers also.

Psalms 19:   Child birth:
Danger at childbirth. Pray seven times over dust from cross roads, place on parchment and write first five verses and lay same on the abdomen of patient. Holy name is HE. Use also your own prayers.

Psalms 24, 25: Protection:
For protection, pray daily holy name ELI also psalms 26 for protection. Holy name is ELOHE. Use same along with you own prayer.

Psalms 29:   Evil Spirit:
Against evil spirit, pray daily ten times. Holy name AHA. Use along with your own prayers.

Psalms 32:   Money, Grace & Love:
Pray daily for money, grace and love, along with your own prayers.

Psalms 33:   Death at Birth:
Child death at birth. In future pray this psalm over olive oil. Holy name JEHOVAH anoint wife and use own suitable prayer.

Psalms 35:   Revengeful people:
To be used against revengeful, quarrelsome people and to find favor from all types of persons. Pray three successive days early mornings. Holy name JAH. Use also with you own prayers.

Psalms 37:   Drug Abuser:

If drunken, use this over water, then bathe face and head and give to drink.

Psalms 38, 39: Slander & find favor from all:

For slander and to find favor from all men. Pray seven times in open field, early in the mornings and fast for the day. Holy name is AHA and HE. Use your own suitable prayers also.

Psalms 40:   Evil Spirit:

Holy name is JAH, use daily against evil spirit.

Psalms 41, 42, 43, & 44:   Enemies:

To be used against all enemies Pray 3 times for 3 successive days.

Psalms 45, 46: Peace & Love

For peace and love between man and wife, man to pray over olive oil and anoint body. Woman use # 46 as per above. Holy name is ADOHAH.

Psalms 47:   Favor from all:

For favor from all, pray seven times daily.

Psalms 48:   Enemies:

Against enemies, pray daily. Holy name is SAEH.

Psalms 14:   Slander & Mistrust:

Against slander and mistrust. Pray with holy name EEL SUMMET, over olive oil and anoint face and hands also say psalms 31. Holy name is JAH.

Psalms 15:   Evil spirit:

Against evil spirit, fill new pot with spring water and pronounce holy name IALI with you prayer and read psalm 29, pray ten times, use holy name AHA and bathe person. Psalms 53, 54, and 55 against your enemies pray daily. Holy name 53-Ai, 54-JAH, 55-VAH along with your own prayers against enemies.

Psalms 56:   Passion:
               Read and pray against passion.

Psalms 59:   Tempted to do Evil:
               When tempted to do evil and to overcome same, pray from second verse early noon and evening. Holy name is PALTIOEL, use your own prayer also.

Psalms 94:   Enemies:
               Against enemies. On Monday go to open field, put incense in mouth and turn to east and repeat psalms 94, then to West repeat psalms 92 seven times each, use holy name EEL KANNO TAF with your own prayers.

Psalms 96, 97: Happiness & contentment:
               Pray three times daily to bring joy and happiness and contentment in the family. Holy name is JAH and uses your own prayers also.

Psalms 95:   Unity & Peace:
               Pray for unity and peace between families. The holy name is JAH also against your enemies along with your own prayers.

Psalms 101:   Evil Spirit:
               This can be used against evil spirit and people, write on parchment psalms 101 and 68 then place on the person affected along with your own prayers.

Psalms 100:   Enemies:
               Pray several days, seven times holy name is JAH to be used against enemies along with your own prayers.

Psalms 102,103: Barron Women:
>   Baron women must repeat with holy name JAH and
>   AHA along with you own prayers.

Psalms 105, 106 & 107: Fever:
>   To be used against fever. Pray and use holy name JAH
>   along with your own prayers.

Psalms 110, 111: Enemies:
>   To be used against the enemies. Holy name is Jah,
>   also use your own prayers.

Psalms 117: Forgiveness:
>   Fail from a promise, pray for forgiveness with your
>   own prayer.

Psalms 125: Enemy:
>   If you are going into an enemy city, or house, take
>   two hands full of salt and pronounce psalms over it
>   seven times then scatter into the air towards 4 corner
>   of earth.

Psalms 120: Gain Favor:
>   To gain favors, pray 13 times psalms 127, avoid evil
>   write on parchment and hang on neck of new born
>   son.

Psalms 128: Security:
>   To be secured, write on parchment and hang on body
>   of pregnant woman.

Psalms 132: Broken Promises:
>   Broken promises, pray three times morning and evening
>   for forgiveness along with your own prayers.

Psalms 133,138: Gain Love & trust:
>   Pray to gain love and friendship

Psalms 134:   Education:
     For students to be successful at school

Psalms 135, 136: Forgiveness:
     If willful sinned, pray for forgiveness.

Psalms 137:   Enemies
     Against enemies pray daily.

Psalms 139, 140: Marriage:
     To preserve marriage and love.

Psalms 142, 143, 44: Pain:
     Use for pains in the hands and feet.

Psalms 144, 145: Evil:
     To drive away evil spirit.

Psalms 147:   Stings & Bites:
     For poisonous stings and bites.

Psalms 150:   Praise & thanks:
     For praise and thanks to God.

Psalms 4:   Unfortunate event:
     If unfortunate, Pray three times before sunrise, Holy
     name is JIHEJE also your own prayers.

Psalms 5:   Favor from all men:
     To find favor with all men, high and low—Pray at
     sunrise and sunset three times over olive oil and anoint
     face, hands and feet. Holy name to use CHANANJAH.
     Use own suitable prayers also.

Psalms 11:   Slander & Persecution:
     Against slander and persecution, pray daily, holy name
     is PELE, Psalms 31 to be used against slander. Pray

over olive oil and anoint face, feet and hands. Holy name is JAH. So also is Psalms 36, and 52. Pray daily in the mornings.

Psalms 51:   Forgiveness:
For forgiveness of sin, pray daily at noon and evening over poppy oil three times each. Holy name DAM. Also us your own prayers.

Psalms 57 65: Unfortunate
Unfortunate—pray daily in mornings. Holy name Chai and use Psalms 57 & 65-Jah.

Psalms 60:   Soldiers:
For soldiers, pray daily with your own prayers. Holy name JAH.

Psalms 61:   Possession of new house:
For the possession of a new dwelling house. Bless it and use holy name SCHADDAI, with your own prayers, before entering building and while going in for the first time.

Psalms 62; Forgiveness:
For forgiveness of sins. Use holy name ITTANI with your own prayers

Psalm 63:   Conflicts:
When you and your business partner cannot get along. Holy name JACH along with own suitable prayers.

Psalms 64:   Travelling:
If travelling at sea, use psalms 66. For evil water spirit, write on parchment and hang on person and read psalm 69, verse 2, with hands over sick head.

Psalms 72:   Favor:
Favor with all men. Write on parchment and hang around neck. Holy name ELOHIM.

Psalms 71:   Prisoners:
             Prisoner to use seven times daily.

Psalms 85:   Friendship:
             Reconcile friendship, go to open field, turn face to
             south and repeat seven times holy name VAH.

Psalms 89:   Sick:
             For sick, pour olive oil over ram's wool and while
             praying psalm, raise eyes towards heaven and bathe
             sick.

Psalms 90:   Evil Spirits:
             To be used against evil spirits, pray with holy name
             SCHADDEI also psalm 61 to be used, the holy name
             is EEL SCHAFFEI.

VAN: 41-48: Serving Master:
             Repeats over water and drink—will serve master
             faithfully.

ZAIN: 49-56: Sin:
             If sin, repeat eight times. For sickness write Raphael
             and place on spleen.

OBETH: 57-64: Sick:
             Repeat over wine seven times and give it to sick person
             to drink.

TETH: 65-72:   Pain In Kidney & Liver:
             For pain in the kidney, liver and hips, repeat over
             sick.

JOD: 70-80: Blessings:
             Pray morning for God's blessings.

CAPH: 81-88:   Healing Relationship:
             Pray ten times on score to heal

LAMED 89-96: Favor:
> Find favor from men.

MEM: 97-104: Paralysis:
> On paralysis, prays three successive days.

NUM: 105-112: Travelling
> Pray when going on a journey.

SAMECH: 113-120, favor:
> For favor from all pray daily.

AIN: 121-128, Pain in the limbs:
> For pain in left limb pray daily.

PE: 129-136: Swelling in the body:
> For boils and swelling pray daily.

TSADDI: 137-144: Fair Judgment:
> To give fair judgment, pronounce three times before.

KAPH: 145-152: Injury:
> For injury, pronounce three times over rose-oil before
> anoint.

RESH: 152-160: ear pain:
> Pronounce over juice and put in ear one drop.

SCHIN: 161-168: anoint Head:
> Pronounce over olive oil three times and anoint
> headache.

JAN: 169-176, Left ear:
> Pronounce over onion juice and out one drop in left
> ear.

Because I anticipate criticism from religious leaders on the
section that may summarized as somewhat superstitions I will

now venture to give you the meaning of the word from both the secular and religious dictionaries and from it you, will see, that all persons are included in the interpretations. There is not room for accusations.

Superstitions: A standing still, over or near a thing in amazement, wonder, dread from one who stands by or in present above and casual of. Any believe or attitude, that is inconsistent with the known laws of science or with what is generally such or belief in charm, omens, super-natural etc. Any action or practice based on such belief or attitude collectively.

Miracle: This is an event or effect that apparently contradicts known scientific laws and is hence, thought to be due to a supernatural causes, especially to an act of GOD.

Magic: wonder working in some way beyond the ordinary powers of man.

Amenorrhea: Absence or stoppage of menstruation called a missing period.

Aphrodisiac: Any drug event or practice that increase or improve sexual pleasure. Seen in almost everyday publication is advertisement from one kind or another which claims credit to a new discovery to the human race. These claims also include impotence cure. Remember without reproduction, the human race will surely vanish.

Balanitis: Inflammation of the head of the penis.

Bestiality: Sexual intercourse with animals.

Castration: Removal of the male testicles and or penis for the female removal or destruction of the ovaries.

Change of life or Memopause: Or climacteric the time when normal menstruation ceases. End of childbearing period. It could take place between forties and fifties.

Clitoris: The erectile female sex organ.

Cervicetus: Inflammation of the neck of the womb.

Coctus: Sexual intercourse fornication.

Contraception: Prevention of conception, birth control.

Dysmenorrhea: Painful menstruation.

Ejaculation: Emission of semen from the penis.

Erection: Enlarged rigid penis of the male and the clitoris of the female under stimulation.

CHAPTER 28

Conclusion

The scope of this work, though this book has so far been now fulfilled although, by no means, it is claimed to be exhausted, completed or closed. There is always room for improvements with new ideas and discoveries from time to time. Nevertheless, the facts herein are indispensable.

My suggestions therefore, is that the interested student for that is what you are, should now examine and re-examine his or herself, read and re-read fully to discover his or her individual weak points and to place them alongside the appropriate section in the book. The solution could and would be found depending how tactful and observant you are and having studied them carefully then select your needs and apply them with confidence for the failure or success, now rest with you.

The difficult paths to your problems have been indicated, you are to identify them and with determination, practice and frequencies to the various sections of the book, this will soon be found a reasonable matter to solve. For it will be at your fingertips. Remember your problem no matter how complicated, it may appear at first with the given advice in mind you will be well on the way to complete understanding of the knowledge achievements of what appeared to be earlier a hopeless failure would then, turn out to be a joyful success.

Should you perhaps come across any part of this book distasteful, I wish to apologize for it. I have no intention to be disrespectful, disgraceful or vulgar but rather I did my selection of materials that to my opinion the best and attractive enough to assist the sufferer along the many areas of their shortages and to inject knowledge where there is lacking the kind of thrill which is exceptionally necessary to you. No evil or harm is meant but rather total goodness.

Here, I have summarize, quite briefly the closed scenery of this work as to how you are to act, look for and practice, for your own pleasure and achievements. No matter what is said and done, no book will ever provide you with the several experiences that are necessary for an enjoyable sexual life. This has to be firmly developed by your own practices and experiments with trials, failures and ultimately success. The old saying "try and try again, and you will succeed at last", is a good watch phrase.

The many good books you may want to read on this subject will not provide the technique and skills which are worthy to acquire if one is to enjoy and have full satisfaction in sexual pleasures and not to be defeated and have regrets. They may have attractive guides and could be helpful, but your careful manipulation with your personal touches here and there will contribute and cause you to come out on top of the art with flying sexual flag.

You must bear in mind, that what may be good for one, may not be good for the other, and you will have to diagnose this on your partner and use the method that is appreciate most. The extent and sequence of mutual pleasure is one which each couple evolves uniquely for themselves and each particular partner has to discover the erotic or sexual sensitive areas of the other.

All of us differ, in our physiological reactions to outside stimuli, because of our different personalities and make up, different cultural background, environmental experiences and so on. For this reason, one cannot be sure that what has worked well for many will work exactly the same way for you. All intelligent sexual intercourse and manipulations must be individualized. The best you could extract, is based on reliable experiment and observations, as the old drinker's proverb goes "take a shot and wait for the result" no one knows which shot will get you drunk. As it is, nobody can foretell in which individual you will fail or succeed.

Remember whatever you should do sexually in your bed cannot and will not be evil or vulgar, nor is there any reason to be ashamed, but beware, should the same bedroom actions be done in the open, to the scene of anyone, or the public, it will be regarded as a shameful vulgarity.

Now the magnificent curtain falls, as it will have to on the last scene of this marvelous drama. The reader, in suspense should by now be overcome with the delightful motion depicting the love scenery, which will blind without failure the good referred to herein and even in the hereafter, where there are no regrets.

While on the other hand, if it is on the note of sadness and woeful sorrow, then the heart shall remain without forgetting the stabbing blows from sharp weapon. My experience proceeds expression that is as we experience the truth, we could afterwards express it and in this case, it is about LOVE, HEART-BREAK and overwhelming DESPAIR.